A BREWERYTOWN KID GROWS UP,
PART 2

A Brewerytown Kid Grows Up, Part 2

By: Michael J. Contos

©2022 by Michael Contos

All rights reserved. This book or any portion thereof may not be reproduced or used in any manner whatsoever without the express written permission of the publisher except for the use of brief quotations in a book review.

ISBN: 978-0-578-34581-9

Dedicated to Denalia Jewel Contos

Table of Contents

Introduction · ix

I. The Early Years · 1
   Remembering the Scars We Got as Kids · · · · · · · · · · · · · · · · · 2
   "Forget the Alamo" Devastates Childhood · · · · · · · · · · · · · · · · 4
   Lucky Pop Left New York for Philadelphia · · · · · · · · · · · · · · · · 6
   Recalling a Few of My Favorite Things! · · · · · · · · · · · · · · · · · · · 8
   Father Koenig's Life Lessons at St. Ludwig's · · · · · · · · · · · · · · · 11
   Got a Ghost Tale for This Halloween? · · · · · · · · · · · · · · · · · · · 13
   Blast from the Past: Nuclear Bomb Desk · · · · · · · · · · · · · · · · · 15
   Off to Work: A Message from the Ages · · · · · · · · · · · · · · · · · · 17
   Love Beads Cover My Wicked-Cool Protest · · · · · · · · · · · · · · · 20

II. The Teenage Years · 21
   The Printer's Life for Ben Franklin and Me! · · · · · · · · · · · · · · · 22
   All-Time Favorite Car—a 1957 Chevy! · · · · · · · · · · · · · · · · · · 24
   Highlights of an Early Life Recalled Now · · · · · · · · · · · · · · · · · 26
   Famous People Met: Tale of Our History · · · · · · · · · · · · · · · · · 30
   Writing Frees Us Up for Past Recollections · · · · · · · · · · · · · · · 33

III. Young Adult · 35
   Tales from My State Capital Adventures · · · · · · · · · · · · · · · · · 36
   Karma Enlightens *Groundhog Day* Movie · · · · · · · · · · · · · · · · 38
   Sharing a Little Mysticism from Days of Old · · · · · · · · · · · · · · 40
   Kids Who Shared a Kiss Reunite Years Later · · · · · · · · · · · · · · 43
   Love's First Kiss Lasts…Forevermore · 45
   First Love Found, Never Lost a Heartbeat · · · · · · · · · · · · · · · · 47
   Youth Recaptured through Football Hurdle · · · · · · · · · · · · · · · 49

    Shining Moment Sends Me Soaring High · · · · · · · · · · · · · · · · · 51
    A Twelve-Year-Old's Shining Moment · · · · · · · · · · · · · · · · 53
    Padre Pio's Miracle Work at Barto, Pennsylvania · · · · · · · · · · · 55

IV. Jury Trial Attorney Misadventures · 57
    Reliving the Moment Innocence Is Found · · · · · · · · · · · · · · · · 58
    Closing Argument Opens My Trial by Jury · · · · · · · · · · · · · · 60
    Court Antics: Young Abe Lincoln and Me · · · · · · · · · · · · · · · 62
    "Stagger Lee" Helps Me Win a Dicey Jury Trial · · · · · · · · · · · · · 64
    My Atticus Finch Moment in Philadelphia · · · · · · · · · · · · · · · 66

V. Back Home in Conshohocken, Pennsylvania, of USA · · · · · · · · · · · 69
    Protesting: A Great Democratic Right! · · · · · · · · · · · · · · · · · · 70
    Synchronicity Hits My Home and My Heart! · · · · · · · · · · · · · 73
    Treasures Discovered on My Daily Jaunt · · · · · · · · · · · · · · · · 75

VI. Veterans and the Vietnam War · 79
    "Welcome Home" This Veterans Day 2018 · · · · · · · · · · · · · · 80
    August 22: We'll Never Forget Patty Ward · · · · · · · · · · · · · · · 82
    Confession of an Army Dog Tag Deserter · · · · · · · · · · · · · · · 84
    An Officer and a Gentleman Recalled · · · · · · · · · · · · · · · · · · 86
    Grateful for Choosing the Veteran's Way · · · · · · · · · · · · · · · · 89
    Holidays Are "Downers" for Some Vets · · · · · · · · · · · · · · · · · 91
    Overcoming Fear in the Wild Blue Yonder! · · · · · · · · · · · · · · 93
    Big Lebowski Highlights Veterans' PTSD · · · · · · · · · · · · · · · 94
    My Vietnam War Book Is Finally Published · · · · · · · · · · · · · · 96
    Vietnam War Book Review a 4-Stars Rate! · · · · · · · · · · · · · · · 98
    14 Comments on "Vietnam War Book Review a 4-Stars Rate!" · · 101

Introduction

This book is part two of a series of stories I wrote over the years for my blog. *A Brewerytown Kid Grows Up!* was published in 2017, and this title is a continuation of posts I have written since then. My blog is located at Contoveros.Wordpress.com.

Part two contains more stories of me growing up as a kid in North Philadelphia, taking part in such games as "buck-buck" and "halfies," as well as playing hooky in three different schools and getting caught in two of 'em. I also learned how to box from a Catholic priest who put the gloves on me while a kid two years older than me kicked my butt. (I never cried or complained however. That stems from the Brewerytown kid inside of me!)

The book also presents details of my first job as a messenger boy working out of center-city Philadelphia and shares several pictures of me—at my senior prom, serving as an "angel" for second graders receiving their first Holy Communion, in full uniform at stateside, and even a rare photo of this former first lieutenant in a field in a war zone we called Vietnam.

In addition, there are several stories of my jury trial adventures and how I had some things in common with a young Abraham Lincoln, as well as Atticus Finch, my favorite lawyer character from the book *To Kill a Mockingbird*, as played in the movie by Gregory Peck.

By the end of the book, I return to my veteran status and discuss how I became an officer and a gentleman. At twenty, I was the second youngest second lieutenant to graduate from my Officer Candidate School class of 1969 in Fort Benning, Georgia.

This book also shares how on the actual fiftieth anniversary of my last day in the combat zone—July 18, 1971—I submitted my Vietnam War book to an editor for self-publication. I also added a dynamite review and the responses of many of my actual personal friends and blog readers, as well as my Facebook friends.

I.
THE EARLY YEARS

Remembering the Scars We Got as Kids

I REMEMBER...CUTTING THE BACK OF my hand while running beneath the boardwalk in Atlantic City. It is the earliest memory I can recall. I couldn't have been any more than three or four and cannot for the life of me remember anything else I had done at that moment in time.

I fell while running in the sand and must have stuck my hand out to break the fall. There was glass from a broken soda bottle (an old Coca-Cola green-glass fragment) that rested in the sand and cut right through the back of my hand.

Nothing except for intense pain and crying registers after that. Other than busting through the birth canal one month premature, it was the first time I experienced pain. Years later, I wonder why the most painful moments in my life seem to stick out the most.

I'll never forget how Sister St. Clair had knocked me down a flight of steps at St. Ludwig's elementary school when I refused to "rat out" the seventh grader I had played hooky with. The nasty nun kept pointing her bony finger at my chest as she backed me up at the top of a stairway until there was no room behind me. I had to step back to get away from her, and I fell. Luckily, I was not injured. (See https://contoveros.com/2010/08/12/i-confess-cut-school-with-franny-oneill/.)

I again played hooky at Bishop Neumann High School in South Philadelphia my freshman year and got caught. I was suspended and got twenty days of detention but got it reduced to ten days by kneeling for the hour of detention, as opposed to sitting.

But I never got caught playing hooky at Dobbins Technical High School in North Philadelphia, which was directly across the street from the old

Connie Mack Stadium. After that, I figured I had learned to beat the system and never played hooky again in any endeavor the rest of my life.

I remember singing with a doo-wop group for a dance show sponsored by Channel 29 when I was seventeen but cannot remember for the life of me ever watching the show when the group, called the Five Jaunts, attended a party in our honor the evening the broadcast was aired.

It was one of the highlights of my life, and I'll never forget this cute little redhead from the Greater Northeast who was a "groupie" who liked me. She was attending the party in Brewerytown with other girls who swooned over us young rascals. But I lost all memories of watching the performance, and they now exist only in some black hole somewhere.

I feel lucky because the lead singer's wife had gotten a copy of the audio of the show. She placed it on a CD and made copies for us. I played it several times for my son, Nicholas, and he enjoys it.

I remember when Nick was two or three, and he fell down my neighbor's concrete steps. He received a deep gash on his forehead. We never took him to a doctor but patched it up with adult-sized Band-Aids. The scar still remains, and at age twenty-five, he remembers it as if it were yesterday.

I only hope he can remember playing the guitar and singing lead with the girls and boys in a rock band when he was fifteen. I'm sure it was one of his highlights and that he can remember it nowadays. I wish, however, that I could only remember where I put the pictures that we took of him performing onstage.

Now that would be totally memorable.
(Thanks for the prompt from my writers' group, Just Write.)
(See: https://creativelightfactory.org/just-write/)

"Forget the Alamo" Devastates Childhood

My reality took a major hit when I learned of a book that reveals the famous battle at the Alamo in Texas was not what Walt Disney had broadcast on TV but was a nefarious cover-up of an expansion of slavery in the Lone Star State.

Santa Anna's Mexican troops were trying to stamp out slavery in its territory. The 180 people fighting at the old Spanish mission in San Antonio were trying to not only retain slavery but also make it grow to increase the production of cotton.

The authors of *Forget the Alamo: The Rise and Fall of an American Myth* were scheduled to speak at a conference in Austin in August of 2021 when Texas Governor Greg Abbott forced the gathering to be canceled. He might have quashed it because the book focuses on the history of Texas and how slavery was part of its birth and was included in the original state constitution.

The Mexicans opposed slavery after fighting against the imperial government of Spain. Our southern neighbors had banned slavery outright in 1829. Texans in the mid-1830s, however, wanted slavery to grow, especially after the invention of the cotton gin that made it immensely profitable for slaves to harvest cotton crops for their owners.

The fight at the Alamo was not about patriots fighting against oppression by a foreign power.

It was over slavery.

Plain and simple.

Davy Crockett, Jim Bowie, and William B. Travis—heroes portrayed in the 1955 Disney television series—fought for and were on the wrong side of history. The real-life stories mentioned in the book are unflattering and somewhat despicable, to say the least.

I wanted to kick somebody or tear up something when I learned of the history. And I would have if I still owned the little coonskin hat or buckskin jacket I had when I was seven or eight years old. I would have cracked open the toy model of Davy Crockett's rifle, called "Betsy," which he was portrayed as swinging at the Mexican soldiers at the end of the thirteen-day siege at the Alamo. According to the book, Crockett, my childhood hero, may not have gone down swinging as shown on television but may have actually been captured or surrendered and executed after the battle.

The Alamo was immediately scratched from my bucket list of places to visit before I die. Upon reflection, I felt sorry for the kid still inside of me who was so easily duped into believing such a make-believe story. "The king of the wild frontier"…"Killed him a bo'ar when he was only three."

I know the truth will set me free and help me overcome any and all of these deceptions in life. And my heart will now be prepared for it in the future.

For a review of the book, see: https://www.theguardian.com/books/2021/aug/29/forget-the-alamo-review-texas-slavery-mexico-burrough-tomlinson-stanford

Lucky Pop Left New York for Philadelphia

IF IT WASN'T FOR AN intervention by an Italian crime boss, I don't believe I would be here today.

The mobster had engaged in such enterprises as gambling, prostitution, and bootlegging. In the 1930s, he ordered several of his henchmen to descend upon a lowly speakeasy where they located one of the employees in one of New York's finest after-hours gin joints.

The thugs, three burly guys with brawny arms, ordered the young Greek fellow out of the speakeasy and into the back of a jalopy at knifepoint. They said nothing during the ride from New York City until they crossed a bridge going into New Jersey. That's where they threw out the fellow and ordered him never to return to the Big Apple.

Or else…

Achilles Contoveros, also known as Charlie West, eventually made his way to Philadelphia where he met a farm girl from New Jersey, and as they say, the rest is history.

Yes, my father had been working as a chef in a speakeasy when he was accosted and threatened with losing his life should he ever return to New York. It turns out that he had been dating a chorus girl, one whose name may have been Gay Orlova. She liked the looks of my dad, who passed for a young Errol Flynn, the swashbuckling actor from *The Adventures of Robin Hood*.

A Brewerytown Kid Grows Up . . . Some More!

What my pop didn't know was that the girl, who was a featured dancer at Hollywood, one of Broadway's leading nightclubs, was also seeing another dashing young Mediterranean fellow.

That enterprising man was from Italy.

His name was Salvatore Lucania, but most Americans know him as Charles "Lucky" Luciano.

Recalling a Few of My Favorite Things!

I WISH ALL OF OUR days could be filled with memories of the greatest moments of our lives. None of mine would go down in history or make it into the *Guinness Book of World Records*.

But each is worth its weight in gold, a treasure of memories that anyone, even a prisoner serving a life sentence behind bars, is free to recall anytime, anyplace.

Let me share a few that rank high on my list of inexpensive, memorable everyday imprints:

1. Puddle jumping.

2. Stepping over cracks. ("You'll break your mother's back!")

3. Seeing a newborn kitten suckle with its eyes closed.

4. First frozen custard "swirled" from a machine.

5. Walking on the curb with arms stretched out while avoiding the pavement and the street.

6. The cool sand beneath the boardwalk after stepping on the really hot sand just a few steps out of the ocean.

7. Seeing the first robin of spring.

8. Watching a Slinky "walk" down steps.

9. Riding a bike without training wheels and watching my child do it later!

10. Playing the card game War.

11. Go Fish, while we're at it.

12. Never finishing Monopoly.

13. Winning the game Sorry.

14. Licks on my face by a puppy dog.

15. Playing tag. ("You're it!")

16. Playing buck-buck. (For Bill Cosby's North Philly former fans).

17. Reaching base safely.

18. Watching *Howdy Doody*, *Scooby Doo*, *Sesame Street*, *Rugrats*, or some other kids' show. (Fill in your favorite.)

19. First sleepover at a friend's house.

20. Pillow fights.

21. The first time staying up until midnight ushering in a new year.

22. First favorite rock and roll songs ("Mack the Knife," anyone?)

23. Getting dressed up for Easter, Hanukkah, Ramadan, Diwali, or Buddha's birthday.

24. Walking barefoot in the country.

25. Getting off school with a snow day.

Father Koenig's Life Lessons at St. Ludwig's

FATHER JOSEPH KOENIG PUT THE gloves on me when I was ten years old and directed me toward the kid who was my size but some two years older. That kid—Billy McLaughlin—kicked my butt. But I never cried or gave up as I swung wildly at him in efforts to land my own punches.

I learned that I could take a punch and hang in there when things got tough. It was a great lesson to learn at such an early age, despite the head-banging I got.

The good priest ushered us kids into the church auditorium and gave us treats for attending church the first Friday of every month during the summer. We'd have fun mixing it up with others from the old neighborhood who were being raised in the Catholic school called St. Ludwig's, a German parish in the Brewerytown section of North Philadelphia.

There was a touch of the old country about the church, with its beautiful stained glass windows brought over from Innsbruck, Austria, at the turn of the century. I recently learned that up to 1958, sermons were given in German, and at one time German was spoken in the school. In 1975, attendance had declined to only 50 families, and the Philadelphia Archdiocese had to close the church.

We were what some people later called "mackerel snappers!" At first I didn't know what the term meant but have treasured it after learning of it. You see, Catholics were not permitted to eat meat on Fridays. Hence, we ate mostly fish. So, the name of "mackerel snapper" was fondly created.

We were not permitted to eat any food the morning we planned to go to church and receive the Eucharist or Holy Communion. In addition, we were not allowed to drink water one hour before receiving the sacrament.

Father Koenig also taught us that you didn't have to be a saint to be close to God. You see, the parish priest had a short temper, and it sometimes showed when he was saying Mass. The lid to the chalice wouldn't unscrew properly, no matter what he tried in the sacristy of the church. As an altar boy, I'd hear him struggle and then witness what some people would claim to be blasphemy.

He would curse.

It wasn't a nasty curse but a mild one that most men of that age would use when things were not going their way. The good pastor would eventually loosen the lid and get back into his priestly role. I learned that I, too, could curse a little in my working life and not feel the wrath of God hanging over me.

Father Koenig would drink a little. I'm not talking about sacramental wine but something much stronger. You'd smell alcohol on his breath when you'd show up for a social event mostly for adults at the church auditorium. It was grand to see such a religious man being so human.

He'd often go unshaven for days on end. You'd see the stubble as you got close to him in his black priestly suit and the white collar surrounding his neck. He looked cool! He was the type of guy who could let it all hang out and not try to impose a strict way of life for us boys to follow.

Thanks, Father Koenig. You taught us how to live life without the fear of truly living it.

Got a Ghost Tale for This Halloween?

My uncle Mike was a grizzly, white-haired Greek who spoke little to no English when my father invited him to stay in our house in North Philadelphia. I don't know if he really was a blood relative. Ancestry.com has him listed as a "half-brother" of my father, Achilles Contoveros. Both were from the island of Nisyros, a volcanic island in the Aegean Sea that was part of the Dodecanese group of islands.

That old, crazy Greek was one of the meanest mother-humpers I had ever come into contact with as a child.

He would yell in his home language, and I understood nothing but his extreme displeasure. He looked like he was one hundred years old as his eyes would open loudly and his voice would continue to rise in what I perceived as unintelligible sentences.

He died shortly before we moved from the house, and I did not returned to that section of Brewerytown until decades later. I had not thought about Uncle Mike—Michael Contoveros, who lived from 1874 to 1955—until I was serving as a public defender in the Philadelphia Criminal Justice Center and an African American police officer approached me outside the courtroom.

He introduced himself as Sergeant Washington and asked me if I ever lived in Philadelphia. It turns out he lived on the same street and was a year younger. He also told me that I had helped him learn how to read when I was in third grade and would sit out on the steps to do my homework. I showed him a few things, and I guess it helped him to get over whatever problems he had with reading. I couldn't believe that such a small act could affect someone.

He then told me that he knew the folks that moved into my family's old house. They didn't stay very long. They soon saw and heard an apparition of a crazy-looking white guy with long white hair and the scariest wide-open eyes who screamed in some foreign language.

It was Uncle Mike still trying to connect with someone who might understand him. His ghost haunted the old house!

I recently drove down Marston Street, where we once lived. The house is no longer there. A vacant lot now greets you where our redbrick building and white steps once existed.

I guess someone thought it wise to help the ghost move on to another existence by removing whatever may have been holding it to this plane.

You may rest in peace now, Uncle Mike...

Blast from the Past: Nuclear Bomb Desk

I WILL NEVER FORGET MY old wooden desk in grade school and the drills we held in order to protect us from a nuclear blast. The nuns from St. Ludwig's Catholic School ordered us to get out of our seats and curl up beneath the desks, where we practiced the silence of Benedictine monks. Someone pulled down the shades over the wide windows of the second-floor room, and we sat for long minutes that felt like hours.

I remember the metal shelf built below the desktop and how it held books. The seat was actually attached to the desk belonging to some other student. It was one of the sturdiest chairs I ever had the pleasure of sitting at attention upon.

The desk had an indentation to hold pencils and keep them from rolling over. To the far right of the desk was a hole that once held a small jar of ink for the more advanced students to dip their pens into. No, they weren't quills but something close to 'em, I imagine. I never saw an actual ink container in one of the holes, but I do remember using one of those good old fountain pens. Peacock blue was one of the favorite colors to write with back then.

The desk seemed to always contain at least one book. A Bible history book. I loved to read the adventures from the Old Testament, particularly the stories involving David and his battle with the Philistines and their champion Goliath. I never got grossed out from reading about the young David chopping off the giant's head or learning how one of my other favorites—Samson—lost his sight as well as his power after his hair was cut. He brought the house down eventually and showed the bad guys that you just didn't mess around with God-fearing people like him.

St. Francis Xavier School in the nearby Fairmount section of Philadelphia held similar desks and periodic drills. Someone older than me recalled how he heard sirens outside of the school one day, and the nun went to the fire escape to see what had occurred. It seemed that for the first time ever, a prisoner had escaped from Pennsylvania's Eastern State Penitentiary. His name was <u>Willie Sutton</u>, who when asked why he robbed banks, quipped, "Because that is where the money is!"

Getting under the desks would do little to help us against radiation from a nuclear blast, I finally came to realize. I'm glad I experienced the drills however. At least I can commiserate with the students nowadays who have "active shooter" drills. I wished we had a world where neither exercise would be needed in our educational system.

Off to Work:
A Message from the Ages

MESSENGER BOY—THAT WAS THE TITLE of my first job when I was fifteen years old. Somebody from the old neighborhood got me hired in downtown Philadelphia, and I took the bus to get to work on weekends and after school days.

I made the minimum wage back then and am so happy at my age to finally tap into those Social Security "savings." I never gave a thought to it until now, while appreciating the benefits from a lifetime of working.

The PTC bus took me to work. PTC stood for Philadelphia Transit Company and was the forerunner of SEPTA, the Southeastern Pennsylvania Transit Authority. I used the buses quite often on the job delivering advertisement proofs that the company, Typo, prepared for their clients out of their offices at Eleventh and Arch streets. (See: https://pennsylvaniadb.com/company/366036/typo-tezvhni-process-lettering-inc.)

We'd walk to many of the locations nearby but got tokens to take public transit whenever the client firm was more than six to eight blocks away. We would pocket the tokens and walk the distance. I viewed the tokens as an added benefit.

I had never been on a train before I started working the messenger job. You had to take the train in order to deliver proofs to one of our most famous clients, *TV Guide*, located at St. David's on Philadelphia's Mainline. It was fun riding the train. None were air-conditioned back then, and you'd raised the windows when it was hot outside. You could also smoke on the trains, something I wish I hadn't started when I was only twelve years old.

I learned quickly about people who would try to con you in the big city. There was the elderly white-haired man who spoke with an accent—possibly Italian—whom I first saw near a bus stop when he asked me for help to pay his fare. I felt sorry for him. He wore one of those old-fashioned 1930s-type hats and smiled a lot and bowed to me when I handed over the change to help him out.

I realized that he was a flimflam artist the next time I saw him on either Broad Street or Market Street. I'd shake my head and want to tell others about him but kept quiet about his scam. I guess I felt sorrier for him than the persons he'd hit up for the money.

When did I actually begin to work as a messenger boy? It had to have been the mid-1960s because I remember hearing a song by the Rolling Stones for the first time. "I Can't Get No Satisfaction" blared out of the small transistor radio. They were cool but not as cool as the Beatles, I thought.

Chinatown wasn't far away from my workstation, although I never ate there as a kid. Nor did I ever check out the old Troc, the burlesque place where women would strip while appearing on the stage. The Troc, at Tenth and Arch streets, also known as the [Trocadero Theatre](), was converted to a music venue in more recent times, but we old-timers will always remember it as a place naughty women would appear to a bunch of lecherous old guys.

I'm glad I worked as a messenger boy. I learned a lot and was able to experience a nice slice of life while growing up.

Working as a messenger also enabled me to make a little money and date my first girlfriend, Peggy McPeake, whom I took to my senior prom in 1966. I asked her to go steady with me, and she said yes on April 11, 1963.

Love Beads Cover My Wicked-Cool Protest

"Wicked cool" is what I thought I'd be when I was seventeen and was about to attend a Greek Orthodox wedding for one of my cousins in Queens, New York. I refused to wear a tie to go along with my suit. Instead, I put on love beads. You know, the ones that hippies were wearing in the 1960s. I was a hippie wannabe. I wanted to protest the institutional requirement to look one way when I wanted to express myself another way. That is, to be in love with everyone and share that love with all whom I came into contact with.

I wanted to be cool. Wicked cool.

Well, my dad argued against it and threatened to leave me at home unless I took off the beads. He was old-school Greek, coming to America when he was only fifteen. He left his island of birth but not its culture. In his world, you didn't disrespect someone by showing up with such a protest symbol.

I put on a tie as we traveled from Philadelphia to New York but hid the beads until we got to the church. That's when I made the switch, slipping the beads over my head as we entered the church proper.

I couldn't believe it. No one said anything about the way I looked or the love beads around my neck. That included my father, Achilles Contoveros, who simply rolled his eyes when he saw me but said nothing to me or anyone else.

No one commented about the beads when I joined in the Greek snake dance at the reception later. My act of civil disobedience and rebellious effort had apparently gone for naught. I simply blended in. Just like the others who didn't care what a person looked like—they simply cared about how I loved them and enjoyed being with them

Now that was cool. Wicked cool actually.

II.
THE TEENAGE YEARS

The Printer's Life for Ben Franklin and Me!

"Here lies Ben Franklin—a printer" is the message gracefully displayed at the gravesite of my favorite Founding Father in the city of Philadelphia. He was ambassador to both England and France, as well as a signer of the Declaration of Independence and contributor to the US Constitution. He was also an inventor, a philosopher, and the creator of the first library, the first zoo, and the first fire company in the New World.

But he chose to mark his resting grounds at Christ Church with a rather simple designation—"a printer." I, too, started my life as a printer, having learned how to set metal type with a hand composition at Dobbins Tech High School in North Philadelphia. I held jobs at three printing places and joked that I once worked as a "stripper." Stripper is the printing term for someone who uses an X-Acto knife to strip away a thin goldenrod sheet covering a negative. It exposes light to a plate that a pressman (or press-woman) would eventually use to create the printed word or photograph on a sheet of paper.

I learned that being a printer could be a courageous job while studying history and the legal profession. It was John Peter Zenger, a printer, who helped journalists of today avoid imprisonment by producing truthful stories about government officials. Zenger published a newspaper article in 1733 that criticized the newly installed British governor of New York for removing the chief justice of the colony's Supreme Court. Zenger was put in jail but was freed when a lawyer persuaded a jury to find him not guilty of sedition.

That attorney was Andrew Hamilton, who obtained the moniker of "Philadelphia lawyer" when he suggested to a jury that the truth should become the defense against libel. Previously, the state imprisoned you for saying anything bad about the government, no matter how true it might have been.

That same lawyer helped to establish another principle in law called "jury nullification." A jury could decide not to follow a law if it deemed it to be wrong. That's what the jurors did in not following the governor's mandate and freeing the printer, thus forging the path for freedom of the press.

I'd like to thank all printers who have provided the world with such courage and farsightedness. That would include that fellow named Guttenberg, who started it all!

All-Time Favorite Car—a 1957 Chevy!

THE FIRST CAR I EVER owned was my all-time favorite one.

It was a surf-green 1957 Chevrolet Bel Air. I paid a whopping $300 for it when my barber offered it to me in 1967. I was working as a printer and had saved up enough money to pay him cash.

It was a beauty with angelic tailfins, making it one of the most distinguished cars ever made.

There were no seatbelts, no console. The front seat looked like a converted loveseat—like a smaller version of a couch. The back seat was even more spacious, although I didn't use it much. It offered knobs to roll up the windows and knobs to increase the volume on your AM radio station (WIBG). The Chevy also provided small windows called vents on both sides of the car.

The brakes were shot. But who cared…?

It was cool driving, man, *real* cool!

I'd pick up members of my old singing group, a doo-wop group called the Five Jaunts, and we'd find a spot where we would croon to our hearts' content without neighbors calling the cops on us along North Philadelphia Street corners. Two of the singers were from Parkwood Manor, in what was known as the Greater Northeast, and we'd meet up at Bridge and Pratt at the Frankford Elevated Line, which was almost midway, in order to harmonize.

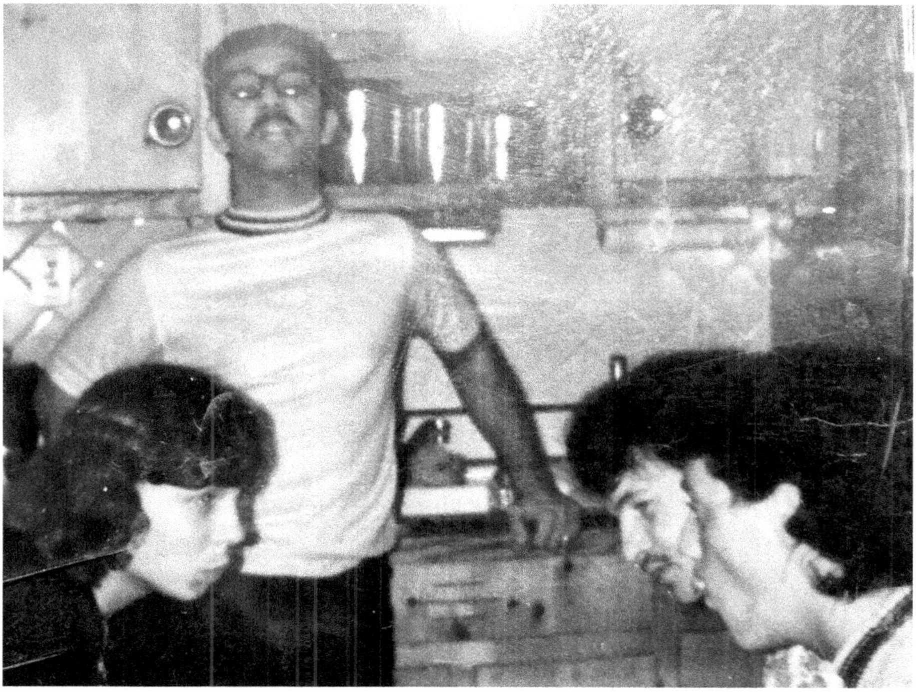

Wearing a white shirt, I sing with the Five Jaunts. Carl Disler is at left, and Jim Hubmaster and Joe Cleary are at right. Bill Kane, the fifth member, took the photo in 1967 right after our television performance on the *Super Lou Dance Show*.

I kept a glass bottle of Listerine in the glove compartment of the car. I'd use it before "tuning up" with the fellows. I'd joke with 'em, wrinkling my nose and making a face when they opened their mouths and suggesting they take a few hits from the bottle.

For the life of me, I can't remember what happened to the car when I got drafted a year later. I'd love to have it today though. What a treasure. What a classic!

Highlights of an Early Life Recalled Now

WHILE I AM STILL ABLE to recall in some detail the highlights of my early life before true adulthood, I decided to write them down for future generations and others who may want to commiserate with my adventures and misadventures.

My early recollection is painful. I was no older than four and was at Atlantic City, a resort town where my Hungarian immigrant grandmother on my mother's side once sold fruits and vegetables and where my Greek father once worked as a chef on the boardwalk.

I crept beneath that boardwalk somehow and remember quite vividly how I fell and cut the back of my wrist. I still have the scar and will never forget the pain I suffered.

My next memory was at age five and in first grade. Sister St. Leonard greeted us in the full black-and-white middle-aged nun's outfit. She was tough. How tough? She caught my brother John chewing gum a few years earlier and ordered him to sit in the wastebasket. She also forced him to stick the gum on his nose while all the other kids laughed at him. He refused to go to school the next few days. It turned him off organized schooling, and he was eventually left behind to repeat the class.

At age six, I was awarded the honor of being an escort for the second graders about to receive Holy Communion for the first time. Sister St. Leonard chose me to be an "angel." I still have the picture my folks took of me in the white cape and outfit standing outside St. Ludwig's Roman Catholic Church in Brewerytown.

I don't remember much about my own first communion, but I do remember kneeling at the front of the church when one of the bishops offered the third graders something called "confirmation." I chose the name of one of my favorite saints—Francis of Assisi!

"Mikie" Contos, age six, serving as an angel for Holy Communion recipients. Photo taken outside St. Ludwig's Church in 1955.

Fourth grade exposed me to the love of history and an eventual path toward getting a master's degree in American history years later. My favorite nun, Sister Josephine Francis, taught us about the golden age of Greece, and I felt a kinship with the land where my father was born. Hey, I'm from Philadelphia and felt proud that my city paved the way for the American Revolution and the creation of a constitution that has so far endured despite efforts by some despots that will go unnamed.

My highlights turned to "lowlight" in seventh grade. I got caught playing hooky for the first time and was knocked down a flight of stairs by Sister St. Clair when I refused to tell her with whom I skipped school. It was really an accident. The fat nun kept pushing her finger at my chest demanding I "rat out" the kid, who was a true juvenile delinquent. I kept backing away from her and fell, crashing all the way to the bottom of the steps.

Eighth grade saw me become a celebrity of sorts. I listened to rock and roll on the radio every night and called in to a radio show presented by the Philadelphia disc jockey Georgie Woods, the "man with the goods." I requested that he play a new song by Little Jimmy Rivers and the Tops called "Puppy Love" that did well locally but not nationally. It became the most requested song of the week, and the DJ played my voice requesting the song on his radio show. I'll never forget the next day when walking into class that a really hot chick way out of my league told me that she heard my voice on the radio the night before. I was thrilled and filled with joy!

(See: https://contoveros.com/2010/08/30/radio-plays-to-my-no-1-hearts-desire/.)

I got caught playing hooky at my high school in South Philadelphia, called Bishop Neumann. He got a "promotion" since then and the school is now designated as St. John Neumann. I was ordered to go to summer school for religion, and my folks decided to send me to a trade school in North Philadelphia instead.

I asked a girl to go steady at age fourteen, and she surprised me by saying yes. We were a couple on and off the next four or five years.

Nothing unusual occurred until graduation at age seventeen. I visited a fellow classmate near Dobbins Tech High School, which was across from Connie Mack Stadium where the Phillies played. No one was home, and the fellow offered me and others a can of beer. We then went to the stage in the auditorium of the school and sat on the bleachers singing "Climb Every Mountain" from *The Sound of Music*. I had to take a "pee" from the moment we sat down, and it was torture to hold it in during the rather lengthy ceremony.

A Brewerytown Kid Grows Up . . . Some More!

I bought a '57 Chevy the next year. It was my first car and my all-time favorite one. I drove it to "practice" for our singing group that I helped form that year. We called ourselves The Five Jaunts and appeared on a local television dance show. I loved to harmonize even though I was never a really good bass singer.

I eventually became a printer, working at two different shops at age eighteen.

The next year I got drafted into the army. I was chosen to go to Officer Candidate School a year later, becoming the second youngest lieutenant from my company at Ft. Benning, Georgia, to be commissioned.

And at age twenty-one, I was leading a combat infantry platoon in the Vietnam War, wondering where oh where had my childhood highlights gone so quickly.

Famous People Met: Tale of Our History

WHO'S THE MOST FAMOUS PERSON you ever met?

I mean directly or indirectly. And I don't mean being in an audience with hundreds or thousands of others at a concert or rally.

President Gerald Ford tops my list. I met him on July 4, 1976, as he took part in the Bicentennial Wagon Train that made its way to Valley Forge State Park. I was serving as a newspaper reporter for the *Pottstown Mercury* newspaper some twenty-five miles away.

I don't remember anything he said but recall him looking out at the crowd after being introduced by the governor of Pennsylvania at the time, Milton J. Shapp. He was one of the other famous people I had met, which happened three years earlier when I was awarded a fellowship to study state government and dine with him and other winners. I also wrote a speech for the governor while working in the public relations office of PennDOT, the Pennsylvania Department of Transportation, in Harrisburg.

Other famous people that I met include both Pennsylvania Senators Arlen Spector and John Heinz. I interviewed Senator Spector at the Sunnybrook Ballroom near Pottstown and covered a speaking event Senator Heinz attended at a high school several months before his fatal plane crash in Lower Merion Township.

More recently, I shook hands with and joked with Pennsylvania Governor Tom Wolf, who took part in a protest against assault weapons at the courthouse steps of Montgomery County in Norristown. He was joined by two county commissioners, and all of us wore orange shirts as part of the protest.

My wife, Wendy, had taken a leave of absence from her newspaper job at the *Philadelphia Inquirer* and worked as a volunteer for vice presidential candidate Geraldine Ferraro as a cavalcade driver. Among those she greeted was Mary Travers of Peter, Paul and Mary, who requested Wendy take her to a famous landmark to get a cheesesteak. They ate at Pat's Steaks in South Philadelphia!

My wife, Wendy Contos, was escorted by my son, Nicholas, as he wore his "wife-beater" tank top while greeting Hillary Clinton in 2008 when she was campaigning at the Fellowship House in Conshohocken, Pennsylvania.

Wendy, who passed away April 27, 2018, played with the youth orchestra in Lexington, Kentucky, and visited the White House when the orchestra played on the White House lawn for President John F. Kennedy. Kennedy told the group he had work to do in the Oval Office but that he would keep the door open so that he could hear them play.

I attended a meditation retreat at a monastery for Buddhist monks and nuns in upstate New York and came within five feet of Thich Nhat Hahn, the Vietnamese Buddhist monk nominated by Martin Luther King Jr. for the Nobel Peace Prize for his opposition to the Vietnam War. While at the retreat, I joined a group of veterans and family members of vets who sang protest songs and shared memories of the war.

One family member asked for forgiveness for what her father may have caused us grunts who served in the war. Her father was a colonel in the Vietnamese Army.

Another woman asked us for compassion for what her father may have done during what was then the United States' longest war. Her father was a military leader of the US Army by the name of General William Westmoreland, who commanded the military operations at the peak of the Vietnam War.

I believe we taste a little bit of history whenever we meet such famous people and their family members. It's also fun to name-drop while showing our own historic roots.

Writing Frees Us Up for Past Recollections

WRITING HAS OPENED ME TO a world above and beyond my five senses. I feel like H. G. Wells whenever I revisit the past and recall what life was like when I was fortunate enough to stop the world for a few brief moments and write about something.

The earliest "something" must have been while I was in grade school. I remember how I wrote about wanting to be a marine when growing up. I was influenced by the marine hymn "From the Halls of Montezuma," and I saw myself fighting for some right as I stormed up the hill at Iwo Jima.

The next dreamlike meandering found me serving as an actor. I'd be a Jimmy Stewart or a Gregory Peck, someone who would appear in front of a bunch of people in a good way to influence them to do some good for themselves and others.

Both of the early writing sojourns occurred while being taught by Catholic nuns. I wanted to "serve," and that's where my writing seemed to take me.

I didn't write much in high school but found myself feeling ostracized and completely different from the fellows I grew up with in the old neighborhood. I felt an empathy for those around me and couldn't understand how my friends could bad-mouth them and try to degrade them for the color of their skin, their religion, or their place of origin.

I wrote a few poems about how hurt I felt and a kind of a sadness that never really got away from me.

And then there was the war and the aftermath that caused such a rage to grow in me years after the wounds took their toll on me. I didn't know it then, but the anger made its way into my very being. I found I could relieve myself through meditation and writing about posttraumatic stress and the debilitating effect combat inflicts years after the mortars stop falling on the troops you once led at the age of twenty-one.

Years later, I was able to write about joyous things like jumping out of an airplane and comparing it to a snowflake making its way to Earth. I studied journalism and found I loved to write—all types of writing, including straight news and editorials. I received a Sigma Delta Chi award for journalism and also wrote a speech for then–Pennsylvania Governor Milton J. Shapp.

My writing reached what I call a crescendo when I was forced to "go out on disability" from the PTSD I suffered in the war, and I started a blog that let me open myself to so many possibilities. Writing has continued to be the lifeline for me, and I hope to continue it in one of my next incarnations.

You ought to try it sometime. Write your own history while you still can remember it.

III.
YOUNG ADULT

Tales from My State Capital Adventures

I ONCE WORKED IN PENNSYLVANIA state government, meeting and writing a speech for the governor and broadcasting a news story about a new group of buses being introduced to the Keystone State.

It all started when I served as editor of my college newspaper, *The Communitarian*, of the Delaware County Community College. I ran a series of articles interviewing county government officials on their advice for an upcoming presidential election. I got high praise from my political science teacher at the two-year college until I—as editor-in-chief—endorsed George McGovern for president, and the professor, a die-hard Republican, chastised me for editorializing against Richard M. Nixon. However, my journalism work was rewarded with a grant to study state government through a fellowship program.

I was honored by the James A. Finnegan Foundation, established in memory of James A. Finnegan, who was secretary of the Commonwealth in Pennsylvania from 1955 to 1958 (see https://www.finneganfoundation.org/). The program provided practical training in government for undergraduate students through a ten-week paid internship in executive agencies located in Harrisburg each summer.

I worked in the public relations department of PennDOT, the Pennsylvania Department of Transportation. While there, I wrote a speech for then Governor Milton J. Shapp, who used it verbatim for a bridge opening somewhere in the state.

I had met the governor weeks earlier at a fancy dinner for the fellowship winners at a hotel in Philadelphia. It was a real honor to dine with him and for him to later use the speech that I had written.

My other achievement while working in state government was to do a voice-over for a television broadcast introducing a new series of buses the state had purchased from Japan. The buses would "kneel" when coming to a complete stop in order to aid the elderly and the handicapped entering the bus. Ramps were later introduced, and it was a real joy to watch the presentation on TV.

I'll never forget how my roommate and I watched the program from nearby Camp Hill, Pennsylvania, and listened to my voice describing the new devices, ending the broadcast with the sign off, "This is Michael Contos, WGOL, Harrisburg."

It was a thrill—a capital thrill!

Karma Enlightens *Groundhog Day* Movie

GROUNDHOG DAY IS A MOVIE starring Bill Murray. His character visits Punxsutawney, Pennsylvania, where he is destined to live one day over and over for what seems like eternity. Its message is one of karma and reincarnation, particularly when one realizes that the director and one of the screenwriters was a practicing Buddhist named Harold Ramis.

Murray plays a weatherman from a nearby Pittsburgh television station who believes he is God's gift to the viewing public. His assignment occurs on February 2nd, when the groundhog Punxsutawney Phil appears and forecasts whether there will be six more weeks of winter based on whether he sees his shadow.

Murray's character has little love for the people of the town or his co-workers, who get the brunt of his disdain. When a blizzard hits the area, he is trapped in the town and rents a hotel room where he awakens the next morning as a clock radio emits the sounds of Sonny and Cher day after day after day.

Murray is "condemned" to relive that day for what seems like forever. Kind of reminds me of the myth of Sisyphus. He was a Greek king that the Olympic gods punished for his self-aggrandizing craftiness and deceitfulness by being forced to roll an immense boulder up a hill only for it to roll down when it nears the top. Sisyphus repeats this action for eternity.

The protagonist in *Groundhog Day* tries to escape this torture of reliving the same day, turning violent and even suicidal before learning to be kind to others and improve his lot through such life-enriching endeavors as learning to play the piano, sculpt ice statues, and love with a pure heart and mind.

He goes out of his way to be kind, compassionate, and giving by saving the life of a man choking on a meal, catching a young boy falling from a tree, and changing a flat tire of a car carrying three elderly women.

It is through these acts of kindness and compassion for others that he obtains his freedom from the cyclical nature of his world. It is the message of Buddhism, whereby a person escapes the suffering of life by being good and doing good for others. Persons "reincarnate" in order to return to another life and "get it right." Students of Buddhism believe that we're all destined to relive events based on the karma we create in previous lives and only the most enlightened among us get to "awaken" and escape!

Harold Ramis, who passed away in 2014, was friends with the Dalai Lama of Tibet. He also worked in a mental institution for several months.

I believe his movies may have incorporated karmic lessons he received from both of those sources.

Sharing a Little Mysticism from Days of Old

I EXPERIENCED THE PRESENCE OF God when I was twelve years old but didn't know it until some fifty years later when I meditated and realized how much the Divine had filled me when I was praying for a girl I had just met on a glorious preteen-age weekend.

I was smitten by Geraldine McFadden, a twelve-year-old who lived at Second Street and Allegheny in North Philadelphia. We kissed ever so gently at first, and before I knew it, she showed me what it was like to kiss as an adult. In other words, she taught me how to "French kiss." (*Please see the noted message at the bottom of this post!)

I wanted nothing more in life than for her to like me. I mean "really like me." And so early Sunday morning I went to church at St. Ludwig's Roman Catholic Church in a section called Brewerytown. I dressed up as an altar boy with a black cassock and a white surplus. I went to the kneeler in the sacristy and knelt and closed my eyes, envisioning what it was like on the night I had met this heartthrob. I began to pray that she would feel the same way toward me as I did toward her.

I prayed, and I prayed, and then something that had never happened to me before occurred.

Looking back, I realized that I had gone into some sort of a trance. I believe it was a meditative state of mind where all thoughts are diminished, and you obtain a clear sight into the place of "nothing" that I read years later that mystics of old had often tapped into.

I experienced a joy I had never felt before. Peace and calm descended on me. I had no worries or thoughts of any past sins and enjoyed being alive in the here and now. I felt unconditional love from the universe, and winning over Geraldine McFadden didn't seem to matter to me as much anymore.

What I experienced was the presence of God, but I didn't realize it until years later when I began to write a blog and started to remember some of the events of my life. Then I remembered that in the study of A Course of Love, we're "taught" to remember who we were in the past—to remember who our true self was and to see life in a way we might have never done because of the busyness, stress of work, and mundane trials and tribulations of daily life.

I was fearful of sharing this with those I grew up with in the working-class neighborhood where I was raised. I felt vulnerable and thought they'd ridicule or make fun of me as someone "different" and too weird to be accepted by them. I still feel that way sometimes. At least the kid in me feels the little "Mikie Contos" inside, who is still sensitive despite his bluster and creds from street fighting and later as an infantry platoon leader in the war of his generation.

I am grateful that I can share my mystical experience without worrying what my old friends and schoolmates would think of me. They might have had similar experiences and are only now feeling comfortable to share it with others. I want them to know that I am listening and will enjoy their story no matter how crazy they think it might sound.

Being present for the presence of the higher self is all that matters.

---

*Note: Nearly sixty years to the date that I shared a famous kiss with my twelve-year-old friend, Geraldine McFadden, she contacted me after her daughter sent her a copy of the original story. It's the one I wrote on December 1, 2010.

She had initially contacted my nephew, Rocky Contos, in California, and my son's second cousin in Cleveland. She was finally able to reach me through Messenger with my son, Nicholas, in Conshohocken.

Geraldine is doing fine. She has been married fifty-two years and once ran her own business, which had fifteen employees. She taught gymnastics and dance and at one time in her life lived in a house she owned in Spain.

I now share weekly messages with her under her married name of Gerrie Menasce.

Now that's what I would call a mystical adventure!

Kids Who Shared a Kiss Reunite Years Later

SIXTY YEARS TO THE DAY of the most memorable kiss of my life, the girl who bestowed that kiss had contacted me for the first time since way back then.

Sixty years!

Geraldine McFadden, now known as Gerrie Menasce, contacted me by sending a message over my cell phone. She had tried to get in touch with me since her daughter alerted her to a blog post I wrote about us sharing that unforgettable kiss at twelve years of age in the Brewerytown section of Philadelphia in 1961. I had written that story eleven years ago, publishing it on December 1, 2010.

Gerrie had lived some ten miles from my home and was visiting a mutual friend who attended the same gym class. I wanted so much to get together with her, but at such a young age, I could neither drive to see her nor figure out how to use the telephone book to call her family to speak to her.

I never saw her again and always wondered what happened to her.

An accomplished gymnast, Gerrie eventually opened her own studio when she was older and at one point had some fifteen people working for her. She taught both gymnastics and dance, and she and her husband of fifty-two years had lived and once owned a home in Spain.

Gerrie had tried to locate me recently by first contacting my nephew, Rocky Contos, who lives in California. Unable to reach him, she then contacted a young woman in Cleveland who turned out to be a second cousin of my son Nicholas, who was adopted in Cleveland, Ohio

She finally reached my son, Nicholas, who sent me the message that led to the reunion of two kids who shared some beautiful moments before turning into teenagers, young adults, middle-aged adults, and...well, let's not go any further.

We have exchanged messages over the past several days, and I look forward to learning more about her adventures. She is in the process of writing her autobiography, and I can't wait to read it.

It just goes to show that you never know when an old (young) friend may hook up with you, no matter how many years may go by!

For a look at the blog posts I wrote about our first contact, please see below:

A "Love's First Kiss Lasts...Forevermore"
B "First Love Found, Never Lost a Heartbeat"
C "Youth Recaptured through Football Hurdle"
D "Shining Moment Sends Me Soaring High"

Love's First Kiss Lasts…Forevermore

First kiss? Can't remember. Must have been a "forgettable" one.

First "French" kiss? Now you're talking. Twelve years of age. At a party in the cellar of the home of Claire Rober, a girl from my old neighborhood but not my elementary school. (Yeah, they used to call grade school by that name. You say you never heard of grade school? How about K through eight, but just drop the K part. We didn't do kindergarten in the Catholic Church parish school I attended.)

I remember the lights were low, and people paired up. An older girl was with some fellow my age, and most of us laughed when we heard her say in a stage whisper, "That's my girdle." I didn't pay much mind. For you see, I ended up with the "new" girl, a gymnast visiting Claire from outside the neighborhood, the love of my yet-to-be teenage years. Geraldine McFadden.

Gerrie was short and compact. She was athletic and wore one of those clinging gym outfits. She was short and brunette, with brown eyes that seem to sparkle and say "smile" each time she looked at you. "She flipped over me" is the story I told later about my first-ever meeting with her.

She performed a gymnastic flip when I asked Claire if her friend could show us one of her moves. She did…right in the upstairs dining room of the small row home in Brewerytown, a working-class neighborhood of North Philadelphia. "Be careful," some adult told Geraldine as she hit the carpeted floor and shook the keepsakes in the china closet.

I loved her immediately. But who knew if it was reciprocal? Yes, somehow, I ended up with her in the basement later. But I had heard that Jimmy Soss, two years my senior and a fellow I always looked up to, had his eye on

Gerrie and made some moves on her. Jimmy was cool. If she liked him more than me, well, no hard feelings. He could have her. You know what I mean?

But there we were, two kids seated next to one another. About twenty other youngsters somewhere else in the old concrete cellar. This was before the days of the "rec room." I'm talking concrete floors, white chalk-like brick walls, and skinny wooden beams across the ceiling providing support and not any form of decoration.

First Love Found, Never Lost a Heartbeat

WHAT WAS IT LIKE TO be a preteen, meeting a person who'd maybe one day be the love of your life? And what did you do when someone turned down the lights in the cellar party…and you were alone…finally. Your hands touched, your eyes melted while looking at the other's face, their smile, their warm and inviting eyes.

Geraldine McFadden and I kissed. Very shyly. We said few words, none of which I remember now. I tried to make her laugh. She did! And oh, how my heart filled up. She likes me, at least a little, I thought. I don't know who moved closer to the other. Maybe it was mutual. But soon we were looking eye to eye, more intently, wanting to take in and remember the magic of the moment. I closed my eyes involuntarily. Was this a reflex move or an action I carried over from a previous life? I moved my head closer. So did she. We kissed a second time, but this time with a lot more feeling, a lot more…love. Puppy love.

"Do you know how to French kiss?" she asked, almost in a whisper.

"I'm not sure," I lied, not wanting to show my lack of manly knowledge. I mean, c'mon. You had an image to keep up, even at age twelve, going on thirteen—actually, turning thirteen in a few short weeks.

Geraldine explained the technique to me. And we experimented. What an eye-opener! Well, lip-opener, really. "Just open a little," she softly said to me, and I complied. What she didn't tell me and what I learned by "word of mouth" was what to do with that small appendage that often got me into trouble from wagging it too much: my tongue.

I swear I did not know what she was doing. I had opened my lips and felt a soft, almost liquid push against first the bottom and then the top lip. Exciting can't describe that first feeling. Try electrifying. Another person, a gorgeous girl who I just met and fallen head over heels in love with, had extended the softest part of her body to me in an exchange of trust, love, and…wait a minute! This ain't kids' stuff I'm dealing with here. This is the real thing—this could be the start of S-E-X.

I don't like to admit it—I don't think most guys would—but up until that moment in life, I never thought of a real-life girl as a potential mate. Oh, I liked girls. But in a shy, bashful way. I liked being with them, liked seeing them smile in my direction, liked to hear them laugh.

But what do you do with them once you get to first base? I felt I had never been up to bat, and here I am, already being walked by a pitcher who is giving me a "pass" to try for second! I'll never forget that kiss. My tongue darted out and made contact with Geraldine's lips and then…we…"soul kissed."

God, I have not thought of that term in ages. *Soul kiss*. That is so "right" for a description. Particularly, when applied to two novices, two youngsters exploring, making their way through adolescence with the help of and through the trust of each other.

I cherish that kiss even now as one of the highlights of my life. But there were two other major episodes that had occurred the weekend I met Geraldine McFadden. Each compete for the fondest memory of my life. And all occurred on one fabulous weekend.

Youth Recaptured through Football Hurdle

YOU CAN RECAPTURE YOUR YOUTH by simply recalling a time in your life when you were your most athletically gifted and soared like an eagle in whatever endeavor you excelled at years earlier.

All you have to do is to focus on an event, one in which you were the center of attention, and recall it in as much detail as possible. Something takes place through your memory recall and your body chemistry that recaptures the feeling you had then—you relive the emotions you experienced—and you can stretch out that feeling for as long as you can sustain it. You will become that energetic, gifted young person once again by simply envisioning your shining moment.

(See description of this psychological phenomenon by Deepak Chopra, MD, below.)

My life's highlight came when I was twelve years old. I was a small, tough kid from a working-class neighborhood. I played "sandlot" football and was picked to be one of the kickoff return players for a group of teens in a section of Brewerytown, a blue-collar mix of mostly Germans, Irish, and Poles, with a growing minority of African Americans. My family were the only Greeks.

Kids from the more affluent adjoining neighborhood, Fairmount, had challenged us to a football game. The older guys decided to play it on the field near Lemon Hill, walking distance from the Philadelphia Art Museum made famous when Sylvester Stallone ran up the steps as Rocky.

I didn't know it, but I was the youngest on either side. I was also reckless and had just begun to forge a reputation for having a lot of heart and for being able to take a punch. I could take pain without complaining and never, ever "rat out" a friend who played hooky from school, snuck into a downtown movie theater, or stole packs of cigarettes from the corner grocer when a customer's order sent the owner into the rear of the store and one needed only to lean a certain way to snatch a pack or two from the nearby counter.

Two of the "old heads," the older teens among us, wore their high school football equipment, with shoulder pads, cleats, and padded running pants. One played for each side. The rest of us played in regular street clothes. Guess who was the only two who got injured that day? You got it. The uniformed guys.

I remember it was a brisk fall afternoon. Leaves had just begun to fall and lay scattered on the grasslands of Fairmount Park, the largest park totally within a municipality in the world. Sun shined through the oak trees that lined the parkway and the streets, veering away from the old Philadelphia waterworks and the colorful "Boat House Row" where Grace Kelly's brother rose to fame. Yeah, that Grace Kelly, the movie star and later-day princess of Monaco, whose bricklayer father was eventually honored by the renaming of East River Drive along the Schuylkill River to Kelly Drive. (John Branden Kelly Jr., also known as Kell Kelly, was an American athlete, an accomplished rower, a four-time Olympian, and an Olympic medal winner.) The field where we played bordered Kelly Drive and was but four blocks away from the Philadelphia Zoological Gardens, the oldest zoo in the country.

In *Ageless Body, Timeless Mind*, Deepak Chopra, MD, says, "Conjure up in your mind's eye one of the most wonderful moments of your childhood…a vivid scene of joy…[with] you…the center of some activity…intensely physical experiences are the easiest to use…By rejoining the flow of one magical instant, you trigger a transformation in your body. Signals…are activated… by memories and visual images. The more vivid your participation, the closer you will come to duplicating the body chemistry of that youthful moment." (See pages 104–105.)

Shining Moment Sends Me Soaring High

You had to be a little tough to grow up in Brewerytown, the neighborhood of Philadelphia I called home the first part of my life. You also needed to be open to other ways of life, different religions, and those of another race.

Many of the kids I went to school with were African Americans. Sometimes, I felt I fit in more with them than I did with some of the whites. I was an immigrant's son, different from the mostly northern European families. I was a white minority, a dark-skinned, ethnic, curly-headed Greek, readily accepted by the mostly lower-middle-class group of Black kids. I learned how to box in the schoolyard of St. Ludwig's Roman Catholic Grade School. Blacks taught me how to jab and punch while keeping my guard up and being able to take a hit, while also learning how to hit back just as hard.

We would not swing for the head but simply slap lightly "upside the head" when an opening presented itself. I learned quickly and soon took on kids outside our school who did not realize someone of my short stature would not back down and would go toe-to-toe with them when they tried to bully me or my friends.

I also learned how to move and use "dance steps" as part of boxing. And just as important, how to "weave" and "fake out" an opponent. Keep in mind, North Philadelphia has given the world some interesting athletic characters. Johnny Weissmuller, the greatest Tarzan of the silver screen and an Olympic-gold-medal swimmer, came from old Columbia Avenue. Joe Frasier, the city's most famous boxer, still provides a gym with his name to train young men near Broad and Glenwood streets.

And Bill Cosby, one of America's best-loved funny men, came from one of the projects not far from my home. He was quite an athlete in his own right, playing collegiate football and eventually earning a doctorate—a real one, not an honorary degree—in physical education from that North Philadelphia university at Broad Street and Montgomery Avenue, Temple University.

It's a shame for all of us who had shown admiration and respect for him to learn how he led another life that dishonors almost everything he ever stood for.

A Twelve-Year-Old's Shining Moment

A FAIRMOUNT PLAYER KICKED OFF, and the football started to fall short. It came right toward me. I caught it, so proud that I could field it cleanly but also have room to run in front of me. Somebody blocked the first tackler coming toward me. I veered to the left to avoid another, running along the right "sidelines" as a fellow from the other side—bigger than me—got ready to make what's called an open-field tackle.

I went right toward him, changing the ball from my right to my left arm and getting as low as I could to the ground, ready to plow into him in an attempt to knock him over. I had "a lot of heart," people said, but they also added I was a little crazy. The tackler got into his crouch, using quick speed to trick me into thinking he was going to hit me high near the ball-carrying hand when he actually "duked me" and went low.

He grabbed for my legs...

And never touched me.

I jumped in the air at the last possible moment, soaring upward, hurdling over his body as he fell face forward to the ground. I was in the air for only a millisecond or two, but it felt like a Kodak moment frozen in time—both legs off the ground, arms swinging in front and back, as I see only a blur to the side of me and toward the front.

I hear yelling, screaming. No, it's cheering! My teammates are urging me to go all the way.

I hit the ground and momentarily lost my balance but recovered and dashed a short distance untouched for the score. I will never forget that moment. Can't remember who won or lost, or even what the score was at the end.

I do remember a friend, Jimmy Soss, retelling this, my greatest sports adventure, to a young girl later that evening. Her name was Geraldine McFadden, whose heart I won the night before. I believe I had solidified my "in" with her through my athletic prowess. It was the second of three parts that made up the greatest weekend in my childhood years.

(Please see chapter 18, "Sharing a Little Mysticism from Days of Old," for the third leg of this weekend adventure with Gerrie McFadden and a look at one of the most mystical experiences of my entire life!)

Padre Pio's Miracle Work at Barto, Pennsylvania

SAINT PADRE PIO HAS A close connection with Philadelphia because of a woman who prayed to bring her sick child to see him in 1968. The blessing he granted led to the child's miracle cure just a few weeks before he died.

The woman, Mrs. Vera Calandra of Norristown, Pennsylvania, brought her daughter, Vera Marie, to meet the friar in Italy, where he placed his wounded hands on the child and caused the miracle the Vatican would later use to confirm Padre Pio as a saint.

The family raised money and helped to build a shrine in honor of the man in Barto, Pennsylvania. I visited there and watched a film narrated by *The Untouchables* TV star Robert Stack. The movie told the history of the Calandra family and how the child's blessing led to the miracle that doctors at CHOP, the Children's Hospital of Philadelphia, could not explain in medical terms.

Vera Marie was born in 1966 with congenital defects of the kidneys and urinary tract, according to medical records. After two years and several operations, her doctors told her mother that Vera Marie was not going to live.

Mrs. Calandra prayed to Padre Pio. One day she experienced the fragrance of fresh roses and then heard his voice telling her to bring Vera Marie to Italy to visit. On September 1, 1968, Vera and her ill daughter arrived at Padre Pio's church, where he blessed her.

The doctors had removed Vera Marie's bladder during one of the many operations she had undergone prior to her pilgrimage to Padre Pio. Their discovery upon her return was a "rudimentary bladder" growing in place of the one they had removed.

In other words, it was a miracle!

It couldn't have come at any better time because the holy man died on September 23, 1968, just three weeks after his blessing.

I remember making my way to the cathedral-like shrine off of Route 100, just north of Bey's Crystal Shop. After saying prayers, I marveled at the beautiful statues in the building. I particularly liked those depicting St. Michael the Archangel, who was Padre Pio's favorite. I visited the museum where there are enlarged photos of the friar, as well as one of the beds where he slept. They even had a replica of an Italian Fiat roadster the sainted man sat in while being escorted from his home to bless those in a nearby hospital.

It was in the gift shop, however, that I received my most blessed surprise. A woman in her early forties was waiting on a customer. Someone who knew her pointed her out to me.

It was Vera Marie in full blossom, helping pilgrims like myself to commemorate our visit to such a site. Her miracle was one of two the Vatican used when it canonized Padre Pio and made him a saint.

She laughed when she saw me kneeling and asked me to rise while giving me a big hug, one of which I will always cherish and remember.

How often can one say they actually embraced a miracle baby?

IV.
JURY TRIAL ATTORNEY MISADVENTURES

Reliving the Moment Innocence Is Found

THE MOST ANXIOUS MOMENTS OF my life occurred when a jury returned from its deliberation room and awaited the judge to ask for a verdict.

The jurist would look directly toward the defense table, eye my client, and then say in a booming voice, "Will the defendant please rise?"

I would automatically stand with the suspect—usually a male facing trial for the first time in his life. I tried over a hundred jury trials, but I could never get used to that heart-stopping moment when a jury culminated its deliberation following days of testimony by witnesses, arguments by attorneys, and instructions by the judge.

I'd get butterflies in my stomach, and my hands would begin to sweat. Fear would strike me as much as it did years earlier when I'd face gunfire in Vietnam and have little or no idea where the enemy was at when first shooting at me.

Nothing physical could hurt me or the defendant while standing next to him, but I knew the words about to be rendered would have a lasting effect on him as much as any bullet could.

There was no rule or law that required a lawyer to stand when the defendant was ordered to face the jury. I did it out of reflex. Hell, I had defended the poor fellow for days on end and fought off assaults from some of the best prosecutors Philadelphia could bring against someone accused of a crime. Why should I not stand and face this final onslaught? Who knew whether it would deeply hurt or greatly help the accused?

The jury never indicated how it might vote when you faced each member seated in front of you as you argued your case. Some would fall asleep. I'd bang the wooden gate separating the jury from the rest of the courtroom to wake them. I'd nod to one or two jurors I thought were leaning toward the defense and would get a nod or two in return, but you never knew how deep such a nonverbal cue would eventually turn out.

And so, it all came down to that brief moment in time. Nothing else mattered except for that precious moment…and everything else in the universe froze until hearing the jury foreman or forewoman say with all certainty:

"We find the defendant…not guilty."

No words could ever feel so free!

Closing Argument Opens My Trial by Jury

THE BEST PART OF TRYING a case to a jury was always the last part, which is known as the closing argument.

I'd begin preparing the closing at the very start of a case. As a criminal-defense lawyer, I would review police reports, witness statements, and any physical evidence that would eventually be shown at trial.

Attorneys develop a theory of the case and that is what kick-started the closing argument for me. I dealt with aggravated assaults, robberies, and drug offenses, as well as a few low-level homicides. There are only a few theories to apply toward such defenses, and I tried my best to fit the facts—or lack of facts—into one of the theories.

Each step of the trial was a part of the closing argument. That included the opening statement, the direct examination, as well as the cross-examination of witnesses, and the decision to highlight a piece of evidence.

There's nothing quite like cross-examining a witness who says something different from what he said at a previous court proceeding. We'd be given copies of preliminary hearing notes and knew what a witness had stated under oath before. I wrote out the statements and almost knew by heart key elements of what they said. When they stated something different, I knew I had them exactly where I wanted 'em—trapped with a "prior inconsistent statement."

I'm sure that you've heard how lawyers should never ask a question without knowing the answer. I believe that is where it comes from. You'd ask questions based on what you gleaned from previous statements. When a witness changed their story, you'd zero in and create what is called an impeachment.

Were they telling the truth before, or are they telling the truth now? How can you believe anything they say?

Such a gift would almost ensure a victory.

I'd write out the closing argument the night before the trial was to end. I'd carry the yellow legal pad containing the argument from the defense table to the jury members sitting in the box. I'd refer to the pad and tell them how I needed it because the case was too important to my client for someone like me to forget the details. I'd use the pad as a prop.

I'd also raise my voice at a crucial moment and then let my voice crack at an emotional part of the argument. I'd apologize for raising my voice as well as getting too emotional, as I tried to appear as humble as possible. It was all true—I'd really get into the closing for the benefit of my client, winning more jury trials than I lost.

By the end of the closing, I'd be exhausted. I'd collapse as I took the seat next to the defendant and hoped my performance won over some members of the jury—enough for a not-guilty verdict or even a hung jury mistrial finding by the judge. Too soon the verdict would be announced, and I'd be back to square one as I started to review my next case, my next closing argument. It was exhilarating and rewarding whether you'd win or lose.

Ah hell, it was always better when you won!

Court Antics:
Young Abe Lincoln and Me

I NEVER REALIZED I HAD anything in common with Abraham Lincoln until I rewatched a movie about the president's early life as a trial attorney.

Yes, Honest Abe served as a lawyer who once worked for the railroads as well as those charged with criminal offenses. Henry Fonda played a young Abe Lincoln in a classic movie on Turner Classic Movies in which the Springfield former rail-splitter pulled a stunt in a courtroom that convinced a jury to find his client not guilty of murder.

A young man for whom Lincoln represented pro bono was charged with killing a man at nighttime in a wooded area. The main witness swore under oath that he was able to see the murder from more than one hundred yards away because he was aided by the light of a full moon.

Lincoln boxed in the man's testimony so that he would have no wiggle room by getting the witness to agree that no one could have seen what he saw if there was no full moon shining at that precise time.

Next, Lincoln impeached the witness with evidence from something called the *Farmers' Almanac*, a written booklet that provided times and dates for the rising of the sun and the setting of the moon. Marking the booklet as a defense exhibit, Lincoln showed in stark detail how the moon had set some two hours before the time of the shooting. The jury agreed with him that the witness had fabricated his story. In other words, they believed the witness had lied, and they found the defendant not guilty.

I represented a young man charged with burglary and assault and used a similar device to show a witness could not have seen what they testified to have seen. An elderly person testified the sun had been up at the time the witness saw the man enter their house and remove items. The person turned out to be the state's star witness, and the testimony came across as quite reliable.

"Did you know that the sun had not risen until two hours after this incident?" I asked the witness during cross-examination. Philadelphia Common Pleas Court Judge Marvin R. Halbert, a prosecutorial-oriented jurist, tried to admonish me by interrupting my questioning and cautioning the jury that my statement was not evidence and should be dismissed.

I then asked for a document I brought to court to be entered into evidence. It was the United States Naval Observatory's *Nautical Almanac*, which showed the exact time the sun rose on the given day in question. I had it "published" to the jury, that is, given by hand to the jurors to review. As they passed it along, they noticed that the sun was not out at the time the witness claimed they could clearly see the assailant.

The jurors could not agree with the veracity of the witness, and they became deadlocked. A mistrial was declared after the jurors reached what is called a hung jury. The case was retried by another lawyer from my office, and it, too, ended in a hung jury. The client was finally set free months later when the prosecutor decided not to try the case a third time.

I saw the case as a victory "of the people, by the people, and for the people," if I may borrow the words from the man who wrote that phrase one Pennsylvania morning. Thanks, Abe.

"Stagger Lee" Helps Me Win a Dicey Jury Trial

"STAGGER LEE," A SONG ABOUT a murder over a dice game and a Stetson hat, was the number-one song in America in the year of 1959. Listening to it, I was reminded of how I won a jury trial by using its lyrics for my closing argument.

The song, recorded by New Orleans native Lloyd Price, told of two men who "gambled late." One accused the other of cheating, leading to the shooting death of the other.

I represented a client who told me he was shooting dice outside of a Philadelphia bar when he won all the money from a fellow who had gambled late outside the bar.

My guy was arrested within hours of the dice game after the loser reported his money lost to the police, claiming the defendant stole it from him. I was able to get the police report, which showed there was more than an hour delay from when the alleged crime took place and the actual call to the police. Most crimes are reported immediately after they occur.

The so-called victim testified that he had not reported the incident until getting home and telling his wife that he did not have the money they needed because he was robbed. It wasn't until his wife insisted that he contact authorities that he called about the theft.

The witness denied having lost the cash by shooting dice but admitted under cross-examination to being in the bar, a place he often frequented. However, he was unable to account for his delay in reporting his story.

I called my client to the witness stand and asked no questions. But I also directed him to roll down one sleeve of his shirt. He slowly rolled down the shirt sleeve, exposing a colorful tattoo of two dice—a five and a two, which made up the winning roll of a seven.

I then published him to the jury by having him stand and walk over to the jury box for the jurors to get a good look at the tattoo.

That tattoo became the winner when the jury deliberated and rendered their not-guilty verdict. They disbelieved the victim and accepted my analysis of the incident, particularly after I told them the story of Stagger Lee and recited a few of the song's verses.

It was the right thing to do, and I was surprised and filled with joy upon leaving the courtroom after the verdict as the judge—James Lineberger, one of my favorite jurists—said to me, "Go, Stagger Lee, go!"

My Atticus Finch Moment in Philadelphia

SHE STARED AT ME AS I walked from the courtroom. I felt her hate bore into me. Her whole posture seemed to drip with contempt and what I could only feel at that moment was a curse from her whole being.

I had just brutally attacked her son, dragging his name through the mud of a jury trial in efforts to show that my client was innocent and that her son was the real culprit the police should have investigated. It was too late for that type of justice now because someone had shot and killed him. All that his mother had left of him were memories of a child she would always love, always defend.

Years later, I would recall her "stare-down" attack at the Philadelphia courthouse as I watched Atticus Finch, the hero from the movie *To Kill a Mockingbird*. He refused to react to the father of a girl the criminal-defense lawyer had shown was a liar when she testified against a Black man charged with raping her. The girl's father approached Atticus, played by Gregory Peck, and he spat into the attorney's face.

Atticus says nothing and refuses to retaliate, as he simply reaches into his pocket and pulls out a handkerchief to wipe the spittle away. The Alabama gentleman turns and leaves but not before one of Atticus's children had witnessed the hate-filled display.

The father of the man charged with the crime looks on with respect and admiration while standing behind Gregory Peck.

My client was charged with a shooting in a poor section of North Philadelphia. I compared his story to the facts presented by the police and used the police paperwork and a touch of common sense to show the law enforcement officials had arrested the wrong man. I even broke with my own tradition of keeping the defendant off the witness stand after deciding that he could tell his story convincingly, with little fear of his failing upon cross-examination by the seasoned prosecutor.

The evidence raised reasonable doubt that he had committed the crime and pointed the finger at the young man who had been killed on the same street months later due to a gang fight involving drugs. The jury found my client not guilty, but I had no idea of the eventual verdict when I left the courtroom following my closing argument.

And that is when the mother of the slain young man approached me and silently cursed me for besmirching her son's memory.

I took the heat. I took the hatred. I took the evil upon myself and walked out with my head held high and my belief in the law intact. Years later, I understood how Atticus Finch felt when he absorbed the hatred and disdain yet felt proud to have engaged in the battle for the truth.

V.
BACK HOME IN CONSHOHOCKEN, PENNSYLVANIA, OF USA

Protesting:
A Great Democratic Right!

I PROTESTED MORE IN THE year 2020 than I had ever exercised that American constitutional right in my entire life and feel really good about my actions!

I protested the attempted curtailment of postal services at the Conshohocken Post Office and knelt for eight minutes and forty-six seconds at the Montgomery County Courthouse in protest of the police killing of George Floyd.

Meanwhile, I took part in a rally against the current president in West Conshohocken by waving banners saying "Biden for President," created by a Hispanic youth from Norristown who was but nineteen years old.

And, as a former combat infantry platoon leader, I felt honored to have joined forces with Pennsylvania Governor Tom Wolf at the courthouse steps in Norristown to protest gun violence.

Today is the anniversary of the world's largest protest ever. It was on October 15, 2011, that global protests were held, inspired by the <u>Arab Spring</u>, the <u>Icelandic protests</u>, the <u>Portuguese "Geração à Rasca,"</u> the <u>Spanish "Indignants,"</u> the <u>Greek protests</u>, and the <u>Occupy movement</u>.

I had taken part in only three protests prior to my most recent activities. I felt it was my duty to speak out and assert my right guaranteed by the First Amendment to the Constitution, which says the following:

"Congress shall make no law respecting an establishment of religion, or prohibiting the free exercise thereof; or abridging the freedom of speech, or of the press; or the right of the people peaceably to assemble, and to petition the Government for a redress of grievances."

My first protest occurred in Philadelphia outside the former *Inquirer* building. I was a union organizer representing the Newspaper Guild and proudly marched in the job action against management.

My next two protests also took place in Philadelphia, a block away from Independence Hall. I joined a bunch of Buddhists protesting the Chinese occupation of Tibet. I carried signs and smiled and waved at motorists who honked in support while passing us in the rain that poured on both occasions.

MICHAEL J. CONTOS, ESQ. PROTESTING THE ACTIONS OF THE POSTMASTER GENERAL IN CONSHOHOCKEN, PENNSYLVANIA, IN 2020.

I feel that protesting is a form of duty, if you know what I mean. As an issue arises, I believe the universe is providing me a way to show my feelings.

It was most rewarding to join my fellow public defenders outside the county courthouse in support of Black Lives Matter and against police brutality. I also took pride as a veteran to protest the use of assault rifles in America.

Like I said, it's a way of doing my duty for God and country. You ought to try it sometime!

MICHAEL J. CONTOS, ESQ., WEARING A SHIRT COMMEMORATING THE SEVENTIETH BIRTHDAY OF THE DALAI LAMA, JOINS PENNSYLVANIA GOVERNOR TOM WOLF AND MONTGOMERY COUNTY COMMISSIONER VAL ARKOOSH AT THE MONTGOMERY COUNTY COURTHOUSE. THEY ARE WEARING ORANGE IN PROTEST OF GUN VIOLENCE IN 2019.

Synchronicity Hits My Home and My Heart!

SYNCHRONICITY IS A TERM I have come to cherish since being introduced to it by my favorite psychologist, Carl Jung. It refers to deeply meaningful coincidences that mysteriously occur in one's life. Jung proved by the law of probability that they were not mere coincidences but insights into our rich and worthwhile lives.

My most recent one occurred when I published a photograph of two of my grandchildren at the Glendinning Rock Garden in the Brewerytown section of Philadelphia. The garden was a favorite spot for kids and grown-ups to visit and enjoy the spring waters and streams that flowed near the current Kelly Drive. Brewerytown was famous for beer production and much of the brew was shipped along the Schuylkill River and transported on land up Brewery Hill Drive, some two blocks away from the Philadelphia Zoo.

I published the photo—taken last summer—on Facebook with a group named "Brewerytown, St. Ludwig's School," which mentioned my elementary school and our old neighborhood. It got thirty-six comments and seventeen likes within just a few days.

One of the comments was from a fellow who rode horses near the garden and across the railroad tracks close to my home on Thirty-First Street near Girard Avenue. It jarred a memory I had as a kid of seeing horses being ridden by Black cowboys over the rough land and concrete grounds near one of the old breweries.

Black cowboys? Yes, Philadelphia had a slew of 'em, but I didn't know that until I recalled the filming of an independent movie with Idris Elba that was released just a month earlier in April 2021. The movie is called *Concrete Cowboys* and was filmed in and around Fletcher Street, some twelve blocks away from Girard Avenue.

It told the story of how many Blacks from the South made their way to Philadelphia in the early 1900s and rode horses and wagons while establishing stables near their homes just north of the Strawberry Mansion section, as well as other Philly sites. It also mentions the famous jazz musician John Coltrane, the great saxophonist who once lived at 1511 North Thirty-Third Street in Philadelphia.

After reading the Facebook comment, I watched the movie on Netflix. This is where the synchronicity flourished and made me smile!

Elba meets up with many of the cowboys who recall the stables and horse-riding locations throughout the city, and he mentions Thirty-First Street—my home street where my father purchased a house for just $5,000 many years ago. Thirty-First Street, where cops had arrested me for pitching pennies (see https://contoveros.com/2010/08/31/corner-lounging-a-way-of-life-in-city/) and later for sneaking into the ACME warehouse to get half balls from the roof. (See https://contoveros.com/2010/05/22/escaping-brewerytown-in-1-piece-not-easy/)

What a glorious feeling to cherish my old hometown and the street where I grew as a teenager, sang doo-wop on street corners, and was later drafted into the army.

Thank you, Carl Jung, for showing me how such connections are inspired by mystical occurrences and joyful reflections…

Treasures Discovered on My Daily Jaunt

I HAVE FOUND SO MANY little treasures on my daily walk as I strive each day to achieve my goal of ten thousand steps.

Yep, I log all of my paces on a skinny Fitbit wrapped around my wrist, which also tells me the time of the day, as well as the number that is calling my cell phone.

I discovered there are little treasures along my trek, and I look forward to discovering them along my merry way. In between, I compliment the people I see. I have made acquaintance with other walkers, including young couples, parents with children in carriages, or like me, lone pedestrians.

Every time I find coins, however, I am reminded of a song or an old-time saying that lightens my steps and provides me with gratitude for the great outdoors.

For instance, when I find a penny on the ground, I think of my favorite Founding Father, Ben Franklin. It was that famous Philadelphian who philosophized, "A penny saved is a penny earned."

If I come across two pennies, I switch to a comment that may have originated in Philly or some other tough urban center. That is the street urchin who always wants to get his "two cents' worth" into the conversation.

Finding three little Lincoln coins reminds me of the hundred-year-old play *The Three Penny Opera*, in which the song "<u>Mack the Knife</u>" was born. It was later sung in about 1960 by my favorite singer, Bobby Darin. When I find a nickel, Darin sings, "Five will get you ten old Mackie's back in town."

Ten cents are part of that song but also depict what James Cagney would accuse a despicable comrade of being "a dirty rat" or in the more modern lingo, "a dime-dropper."

Gary US Bonds comes to mind when I discover a quarter lying on the ground. "I danced to a quarter of three" runs through my mind. I once found a twenty-dollar bill on the pavement outside of a drive-through bank. It had to have been dropped by a motorist who was a little careless with the cash. I also picked up a five-dollar bill less than a block away at a World War II monument on Conshohocken's main street, Fayette Street.

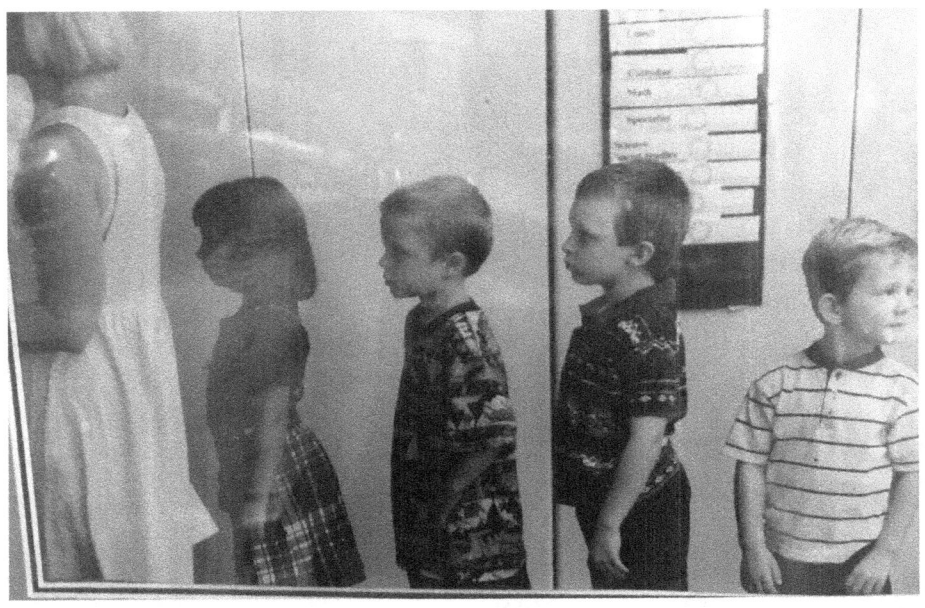

My son, Nicholas, is the second one on the right on his first day of school in the first grade. Photo published in the *Conshohocken Recorder* in September of 1998!

But the greatest treasure was in learning about a photograph that my town's weekly newspaper once used. A reporter was doing a feature story on a kid going to school for the first day. He was outside Conshohocken Elementary School just a block and a half from my home as he patiently waited with other kids being led into the school by their first-grade teacher.

The photographer captured the picture of my son, Nicholas, standing in the line on his very first day of school. The picture ran across the entire

A Brewerytown Kid Grows Up . . . Some More!

front page, and I was lucky enough to contact the publisher and get a hard copy of the pic, which I framed and hung in my dining room.

While walking on Fayette Street recently, I spoke with a fellow in his early forties. He was working for the Coll shop where Conshohocken's former weekly newspaper was published. I thanked him for the photograph that his father had published nearly twenty years earlier. He was sitting outside Coll's custom frame shop. I told him about the connection to my son and how I wish I could thank his father personally for taking the photograph.

"You're welcome," the man said. "I took the picture," he added.

Talk about a treasure. You never know what you're going to find when you open yourself to the little gifts in our universe.

At press time, Nicholas was working part-time at Coll's as a "framer."

(For a closer look at Coll's please see this link: https://www.yelp.com/biz/colls-custom-framing-and-photography-conshohocken).

VI. VETERANS AND THE VIETNAM WAR

"Welcome Home" This Veterans Day 2018

ONE HUNDRED YEARS AGO, PEACE-LOVING people throughout the world commemorated the "war to end all wars" by institutionalizing a holiday that morphed into Veterans Day in America.

World War I, as historians have named it, did not end all of the wars. In twenty years, the nations of the earth faced the worst world war mankind has ever known.

Veterans Day was officially created in 1954, replacing the original holiday that was created in 1918. Armistice Day marked the historic event that officially ended the war in Europe that America had entered into a little more than a year earlier. An agreement was signed by the warring factions just as the morning clock was approaching the eleventh hour of the eleventh day of the eleventh month.

Celebrations were held in the nation's largest cities, and old-timers would later recall where they were when they heard the news, much like we remember where we were on 9/11 or for the older folks, the day President Kennedy was killed. It became known worldwide as Armistice Day. Many groups commemorated the ending of the violence with Remembrance Day activities that corresponded with the honoring of those who died and those who entered into harm's way for the benefit of others.

In the United States, Congress officially changed the name of the holiday shortly after the Korean War ended. Canada and Australia observe Remembrance Day on November 11, and Great Britain observes Remembrance Day on the Sunday nearest to November 11. Armistice Day remains the name of the holiday in France and Belgium, and it has been a statutory holiday in Serbia since 2012. In Italy, the end of World War I is commemorated on November 4, the day of the Armistice of Villa Giusti.

Native Americans honor veterans in a different way that helps them in returning home from the wars, particularly if you're a Vietnam veteran. During a powwow, Native Americans parade in full dress while they conduct a ceremony involving feasting, singing, and dancing. At the very end, they call for all veterans in the audience to join in their circle as they perform their final dance and come to a stop, lining up to shake hands with each and every soldier, sailor, marine, airman, and coast guard member and quietly tell us, "Welcome Home."

August 22:
We'll Never Forget Patty Ward

PATTY WARD, A SPECIALIST 4 with a helicopter gunship, was shot down 50 years ago while flying to the aid of US Army soldiers during the Vietnam War. He was one of four men who died when their helicopter was hit and crashed.

Patty was awarded the Silver Star for bravery in connection with helping to rescue other grunts wounded in another battle. His family in the Fairmount section of Philadelphia received the medal posthumously.

Being drafted, Patty had less than three months left before he was to be discharged from the army. He was what veterans called a "short-timer."

He was the kindest man I ever knew from Fairmount, always helping and lending a hand to someone outside his circle of friends who attended Roman Catholic High School or St. Francis Xavier Church and School.

His smile lit up the room, and you couldn't help but feel he was a long-lost brother who'd give you the shirt off his back even though you competed against him in sports games just a few blocks away from the Philadelphia Art Museum.

Us guys from Brewerytown, another working-class section of the city, played football at Lemon Hill and basketball at what has become known as Boat House Road, both in Fairmount Park, the largest park within a municipality in the world.

I cried like a baby dozens of years ago when I visited the small park carved out of a section of his hometown, honoring him and other veterans who gave their lives for the rest of the nation. I cried when I took my then-fourteen-year-old to visit the memorial site, the first in the nation to honor a Vietnam veteran. And I'll probably sob once again in the future when I take my one-year-old grandson to visit the memorial site along Aspen Street, not far from the Eastern State Penitentiary.

Patty died on August 22, 1968. It was the same year that I was drafted.

It was also the anniversary of the day I was commissioned as an officer in the army before being sent to serve the country in the Vietnam War.

Some five hundred people turned out for a Mass at St. Franny's, the nickname for the Catholic church in Fairmount. About the same number gathered to hear speakers recall Patty's life at home, as well as his last day at war.

I was thrilled to hear that one of my favorite Philadelphia-area congressmen was named after Patty. Patrick Murphy, who was the first veteran of the Iraq War to be elected to the United States House of Representatives, was named after Patty. Congressman Murphy's mother was a close friend from Fairmount who wanted her son to carry on his name.

Patty will live in the hearts of people who have met him, and I believe his legacy of kindness and good will continue hundreds of years from now.

God bless you, Patty.

Confession of an Army Dog Tag Deserter

I CONFESS. I DISOBEYED ORDERS when I marched into combat as a young man, and I want to finally get it off my chest after all these years.

I removed my dog tags from around my neck because they were making too much noise in what soldiers in the Vietnam War called "the bush." I didn't want to let "Charlie" know we were searching for him and his Vietcong brothers. I hid the tags in a rugged duffel bag left in the base camp from where we were shuttled off from by helicopters every two weeks to hump the jungle. I kept them secreted along my personal belongings and a bunch of military paraphernalia.

If you don't know, the dog tags are used to identify a fallen soldier. They are needed to be placed on or near the body of a person killed in combat. They have pertinent information about you, including your Social Security number, religion, and blood type.

I never liked the feel of the chain around my neck. I didn't like the scapular the Catholic Church wanted me to wear either. Nor could I abide with the masking tape soldiers were advised to use to tape the tags together. The tape prevented the metal from making noise and also blocked sunlight or moonlight from reflecting off 'em.

If you've ever gone through basic training, you'd have some idea why they're called "dog tags." The ID tags actually resemble the same type used for dogs. In addition, nasty, old drill sergeants treated you worse than a dog until you'd earned the right to be called a soldier, paratrooper, marine, sailor, or airman.

Why were there two tags? According to an unofficial report, one tag was immediately taken from the neck of the fallen person, usually by a responsible officer, to show proof that the specific serviceman had been killed in action. The other tag remained at all times on or with the body so his or her identity would not be misplaced or lost.

While I never got caught "out of uniform" by not having them on, I eventually lost the tags the last day I was in the combat zone.

A helicopter airlifted me out of a base camp, and I was then assigned to ride in the cab of a truck to get back to headquarters. Someone told me to throw the duffel bag onto the back of the truck where a bunch of other bags was already loaded.

The roads were really rutted and chewed up. The bag apparently fell from the truck, and I lost it and everything in it, including the old dog tags.

Years later, a replica of the dog tags magically reappeared in my life however.

Unbeknownst to me, my son, Nicholas, had contacted the army, got the information on the tags, and had a picture of them tattooed to the center of his chest!

Social Security number included!

An Officer and a Gentleman Recalled

I WAS COMMISSIONED A SECOND lieutenant fifty years ago. Looking back, I see it as one of the greatest achievements of my life, also one of the luckiest ones, and I'm so glad to still be around to talk about it.

Yes, by an act of Congress, I was made "an officer and a gentleman." I don't know where that title came from—Great Britain, I guess—but I tried to live up to its "ideal" while in the army and when discharged and choosing different career paths in my life.

Like many veterans, I utilized the GI Bill to improve my education, having gotten nothing more than a high school diploma, from a trade school at that. I got an associate's degree, a bachelor's degree, and a master's degree in four years, relishing the training I got at Officer Candidate School to "accomplish the mission."

At age twenty, I was the second youngest soldier to graduate from the Fort Benning "school for boys," aka the US Army's Officer Candidate School. The company commander tried to force me out because of my age. He ordered me to do hundreds of sit-ups in a sleeping bag while in his office, but I refused to quit, despite having to go on sick call the next day for injuries caused to my butt during the process.

My brother, Sergeant George S. Contos, gave me my first salute and pinned the yellow bars on my shoulders. He was a "lifer," having served more than twenty-two years as an army combat engineer.

He was the one who talked me into going to OCS when I scored high in a leadership test.

A year later I was leading a combat infantry platoon in Vietnam. Thanks a lot, Brother George!

Twenty-one-year-old Second Lieutenant Michael J. Contos a few weeks before attending "jump school" to become an airborne paratrooper enroute to the Republic of South Vietnam in 1970.

No one was killed under my command, although five guys were wounded one day, the worst day of my life. I am eternally grateful. And when times were bad in civilian life, I thought back to the war, thanking God and saying, "At least no one is shooting at me!"

There was an urban legend that may have some truth to it, but I don't know. "What was the life expectancy of a second lieutenant landing in a hot LZ?" (That's a helicopter coming into a landing zone under fire by the Vietcong.)

"Sixteen minutes."

I never experienced such a firefight like that. But the first person killed when I served in Vietnam was a first lieutenant—Lieutenant Vic Ellinger—shot by an enemy sniper. I'll never forget you, buddy…

Many enlisted men disliked their officers. "Don't call me 'sir.' I work for a living," some officers would say with a sneer. Well, I worked. I walked point in Vietnam, once using a machete to cut through the triple canopy jungle. I would never ask a troop to do anything I wouldn't do. Except carry an M60 machine gun, maybe. Hey, I am 5 feet, 6 inches tall and weighed only 140 pounds soaking wet back then!

The date of August 22 will always be a glorious day for me. I became an officer then and I have tried my best to always live up being a gentleman. I feel blessed to have been given the chance to serve!

Grateful for Choosing the Veteran's Way

I DIDN'T WANT TO GO to Vietnam. Who did back in 1968? I was never a gung-ho type of a guy, even though I'd go a little berserk when a buddy of mine got attacked by some bully at home or in school.

I had been in the army a little more than a year after being drafted. I had less than ten months left on active duty, and I could have quit right then and there and avoided the orders to go to Vietnam.

You see, I was being trained in the US Army's Officer Candidate School at Fort Benning, Georgia. My entrance into the prestigious school was delayed twice because my father had been born outside of the United States. He came from one of the Greek islands and was too young to serve in World War I and too old during World War II. In addition, he did a short stint in a prison called Sing Sing in New York after getting arrested for working in a speakeasy. I couldn't get a secret clearance until researchers could confirm that I wasn't a communist or something that might one day become something subversive like a Democrat.

Well, there I was in the twenty-fifth week of a twenty-six week rigorous-training program about to be commissioned a second lieutenant. I could simply refuse the promotion and remain a Spec 5 (Specialist Five) for my remaining time in the military. You needed at least a year to be sent to the war zone back then. The army would have kept me stateside and out of harm's way over there.

I actually organized a group meeting with other candidates as we discussed our options. We'd avoid facing combat and possibly getting killed or maimed if we quit our training. It had quite an appeal to me, a twenty-year-old from a working-class neighborhood of Philadelphia.

But I figured I had put too much of myself into the army. My brother, a sergeant who became a "lifer" with more than twenty years in the Army Corps of Engineers, believed I could become an officer when he recommended that I attend the school. I had enough chutzpah to think I could actually help others as a leader, and I hated to see the training go to waste. So I opted to be the second-youngest candidate to receive a commission and later tour Southeast Asia as an infantry platoon leader.

I survived the war. No one under my command was killed, although several brave young men—we called ourselves "grunts"—were wounded. And I learned a lesson I'd like to pass on to my grandson this Veterans Day—don't quit to take what looks like an easier path in life. The difficult pathways help you grow up to be more grateful for having served.

Holidays Are "Downers" for Some Vets

HOLIDAYS AIN'T WHAT THEY USED to be when you were a kid. Particularly, if you ended up in the military and spent some of your formative years in a war zone like the Vietnam War.

I could not celebrate Thanksgiving Day this year. It was the fiftieth anniversary of the death of a comrade of mine named Victor Lee Ellinger, a first lieutenant who was shot and killed by an enemy sniper just three days before the holiday. (See Cost of War.)

I'll never forget the anguish I felt and the inability to properly mourn him. The holiday lost all of its meaning years later when I looked back and recalled the events of his death. There were three junior officers in our company. Victor was by far the best, and I'll never forget how the other lieutenant and I ate our Thanksgiving dinner in a rear encampment away from the "bush" just three days after the shooting. It seemed there was little if anything to be thankful for that day in 1970.

Christmas was also bad that year. I had been relieved of my command right before the holiday. As an officer, I had ordered mortar rounds to be fired upon a riverbank where I was leading my platoon and suspected the enemy was waiting to ambush us. The rounds fell a long way off the target, and I kept ordering the sergeant shooting the armament several clicks away to "step down" to get the mortar rounds closer to the Vietcong. (A click is actually a kilometer.)

After three or four attempts, the last round struck us, and five of my platoon members—called "grunts"—were wounded and eventually medevacked out. An investigation was conducted about the so-called "friendly fire" episode, and I was held responsible for the mishap and relieved of my duties.

I'll never forget lying on the cot in a tent in a rear base camp and feeling lower than dirt that Christmas morning. Yes, lower than dirt. At least dirt could provide something useful such as transforming food to grow from soil. Me? I felt I wasn't good enough for anything that holy day of days.

I was given a new command and made good despite another run-in with Lieutenant Colonel Sallucci, who relieved me of my command again but was forced to seek my help when my platoon staged a mutiny when the grunts learned of his action. I was able to persuade them to get into the helicopters and fly into the field rather than get Article 15 punishments or being sentenced to the stockades.

And I was given the honor of a twenty-one-gun salute by my Third Platoon upon leaving Vietnam some six months later!

Let's not forget my birthday, which is December 1. My twenty-first birthday was a most forgettable one. I was stationed at Fort Polk, Louisiana, as a training officer in boot camp. We had an IG (inspector general) inspection the next day, and I remember inspecting the barracks the night of one's most celebrated days and feeling so very alone in the army.

You see, I was a commissioned officer. I could not fraternize with the troops or the drill sergeants. I hardly ever visited the officers club and never hung out with any other lieutenants. I was alone that day, and since then I have never wanted to mark my birthday as anything special.

So bear with some of the veterans you know during these days of festivities and joyful outpourings. Some of us have been marked by trauma and experience events a little differently, and all we need is a single person to try to understand that…

Thanks for bearing witness this holiday period.

Overcoming Fear in the Wild Blue Yonder!

IT STRUCK ME AS I slowly made my way from the floor of the plane and stood in the center of the walkway. There were at least thirty other soldiers on the C-140, a military aircraft that was flying over the field where those of us in jump school would soon be taking our first jump.

It was the smell of fear—not only from me but from the collective outpouring of the young men in front and behind me. We were all going to flee the safe and secure cabin of the ship and pray that our chutes would open without a flaw. We had practiced this for two whole weeks and had run dozens of miles to get into shape to face the fear and put it all behind us. We could do this. We could jump with joy and become one with the universe as we floated in the sky like a bird viewing the vast openness of the land beneath and all around us.

All we had to do was to stand up, hook up, and shuffle to the door. Even if we faltered and wanted to back out, there was a big, burly sergeant whose only purpose in life was to not-so-gently push us out should the fear of the unknown eventually overtake us.

All of us jumped. All survived with nary a broken leg or a broken spirit. All got our wings and will have from that moment war stories to tell our grandchildren about our brief moments in the air. We overcame fear and lived to talk about it.

We all can proudly say today, "Airborne—all the way, sir!"

Big Lebowski Highlights Veterans' PTSD

THE BEST EXAMPLE OF PTSD ever portrayed in a movie was offered by John Goodman in *The Big Lebowski* when his character, a Vietnam veteran, pulls a gun on a fellow bowler and threatens to shoot him for crossing the line and attempting to enter a score in a book.

The camera from this 1998 movie classic shows the bowler slowly approaching the line but pans away before he sets the foot down right before the bowling ball is cast. Walter Sobchak, the so-called "crazed veteran," immediately pulls out a handgun and points it at Smokey before he could write down a score for his effort.

Walter may or may not have fired if Smokey refused to give himself a potentially "illegal" score. You can't help but wonder what caused him to react the way he did.

And then the Vietnam veteran utters what many of us who have been in war can easily relate to in our hearts:

"This is not 'Nam. This is bowling. There are rules."

Posttraumatic stress disorder is what mental health experts call what was once labeled as "shell shock" and "battle fatigue." It affects about 22 percent of those facing combat in the military. "Crazed Vietnam veteran" is what television had portrayed several of them to be in the 1970s. Many servicemen refused to put their military experience on their résumés in order to avoid any wary looks from potential employers.

I never fired a gun in a bowling alley or outside of one. But I have kicked the door of a van when the driver had parked across the white line separating two parking spaces at a pet-food store. In other words, his one vehicle took up two spots!

A Brewerytown Kid Grows Up . . . Some More!

The guy refused to come out when I yelled and screamed at him for such an inconsiderate act. I felt like an avenging angel bringing the wrath of God upon his head when I kicked his door and did not give up even when he got out of the truck, stood a head taller than me, and came toward me in the street. He called me a "fat fuck" and I shot back what are considered to be the worst fighting words from my old neighborhood, calling him a "pussy."

Before any punches were thrown, however, the fight broke up when a bystander edged really close to us and called out for help.

Most of us suffering from PTSD have stories like these. We're actually harmless but want to battle for the right cause when we believe someone has wronged the world in some way and nobody wants to take action.

The Big Lebowski captured that sense of what some of us call "righteous indignation." I'm just glad no one's ever been physically hurt by my actions.

My Vietnam War Book Is Finally Published

It took me more than fifty years, but I finally published my Vietnam War story and the toll it took on me after leading a combat infantry platoon as a twenty-one-year-old first lieutenant.

I self-published with the help of editors who wrote the back-cover description. They used a mug shot I had taken some ten years ago while attending a PTSD meditation clinic at Omega Institute for veterans and their families. The clinic introduced me to different forms of meditation that allowed me to eventually deal with the trauma and view the war experience in a more benign and compassionate light.

Here is a description taken from the back cover:

The memories of a platoon leader become the key to unlocking his salvation.

Michael J. Contos may have survived the tragedy of friendly fire, but the worst days of the Vietnam War were not over. After years of battling the past and traumatic memories with no reprieve for good behavior, this soldier was ready to make peace. After meeting two Buddhist instructors, Contos was able to view his war experience in a different light. With the help and guidance of his mentors, Contos not only gained a new perspective of war but of life itself.

A devoted dedication to those we have lost, a graceful study of healing and enlightenment, and a determined and disciplined meditation on the Vietnam War, *Vietnam War Recall* leads readers on a journey, one battle and one breath at a time.

Much of the book contains posts I had written for my blog on this website called Contoveros.wordpress.com. I searched through the history of antiwar quotes and sprinkled them throughout the book. They include one of my favorite quotes from the Vietnamese Buddhist monk Thich Nhat Hahn, who wrote:

"Veterans are the light at the tip of the candle, illuminating the way for the whole nation. If veterans can achieve awareness, transformation, understanding, and peace, they can share with the rest of society the realities of war. And they can teach us how."

I started writing the memoirs while at a five-day retreat with Barry Kerzin, a Tibetan Buddhist monk who is a physician for the Dalai Lama. See his TED talk from Phoenixville, Pennsylvania, at https://www.youtube.com/watch?v=Q7YskUbEyeY&ab_channel=TEDxTalks.

I felt safe and open enough to revisit the war and see myself years later. I started a handwritten journal that became the basis of this book.

While visiting Omega Institute to deal with PTSD with other veterans a few months later, I started typing the journal onto a laptop computer while meditating with Claude AnShin Thomas, a Zen Buddhist monk who served as a machine gunner on a helicopter in Vietnam. He was helping veterans like me deal with the trauma from PTSD. It was the fourth journey I had walked with him at Omega Institute on a scholarship for veterans.

(See Claude's book on Amazon: "At Hell's Gate: A Soldier's Journey from War to Peace." See review at: https://www.dailyom.com/cgi-bin/display/librarydisplay.cgi?lid=1551).

I dedicated the book to Lieutenant Victor Lee Ellinger, leader of the Third Platoon. We had served together until a Vietcong sniper shot and killed him. I still mourn Vic and at one point in my life visited his gravesite in Staunton, Virginia, and saluted him while laying a wreath at his headstone.

Yes, the war is over, but the memories will still linger on. At least I can finally put this journey's writing to bed and hope some readers can benefit from these recollections.

(My book is available on Amazon: https://www.amazon.com/Vietnam-War-Recall-Best-Worst/dp/0578938235)

Vietnam War Book Review a 4-Stars Rate!

Review of *Vietnam War Recall,* authored by Michael J. Contos at Contoveros.wordpress.com

Post by Kansas City Teacher

Following is an official OnlineBookClub.org review of *Vietnam War Recall*:

LIKE MANY OTHER YOUNG MEN of the time, author Michael Contos found himself in the military, headed to a turbulent region of the world to protect democracy. After completing Officer Candidate School, Michael was deployed to Vietnam to lead a platoon of infantrymen on missions while evading the formidable Vietcong forces. Here, he describes the worst day of his life that led to posttraumatic stress disorder (PTSD), a debilitating condition that would threaten to consume his life and linger for decades; a day so jarring that he would not talk about, even with his family.

Upon returning home, his experiences in combat haunt him, so he seeks the help of spiritual leaders to help relieve the symptoms of PTSD. The story is told in the first person through flashbacks, introspect, and excerpts from the author's blog. Through the narration, readers get a glimpse into the personal turmoil that many of our veterans have to face after combat.

The best part of this book is the intimate and emotional description of PTSD; a young leader, not afforded time to grieve or debrief from his experiences, lives with the nightmares, flashbacks, and anxiety that seem to permeate every facet of his life. These intense feelings are captured clearly by the author. I also love the way the daily humdrum of military life is portrayed, and the descriptions sure bring back memories for this veteran. The cadences, the euphoric feeling when you realize your parachute is perfect, and the anticipation of the return to the United States (DEROS) is very real indeed! A little humor, typical of military camaraderie, is also peppered into the pages of the story; I had to chuckle when I read about some familiar but important advice: never crap alone in the field!

Although the messages are powerful, the book does seem a bit repetitive at times. Other than this, there is nothing negative to say about the story, its purpose and voice are truly a gift to an audience who does not truly understand the realities of war and its crippling effects on our young servicemen, not only the ones who gave their lives but also those who returned bearing unseen scars. I happily give *Vietnam Recall: The Best and Worst Days of My Life* four out of four stars for these reasons. The book appears professionally edited and is divided into chapters of appropriate length.

I particularly recommend this book to readers who love historical accounts of war and those who seek insight from a primary source about mental illness. Those with family members in the military will appreciate the insightful glimpse into the psyche of those who have chosen to defend our way of life. There is some moderate profanity, along with explicit descriptions of trauma and wartime peril; those sensitive to these topics may not want to read the book. For all others, the book is a penetrating account of one man's journey toward healing and peace. All who read this story will undoubtedly be moved by the author's gipping words as he relives the most difficult moments of his life. He speaks for the countless others, who remain silent.

Vietnam War Recall
View: on Bookshelves | on Amazon
(See the link at: https://forums.onlinebookclub.org/viewtopic.php?p=1776053#p1776053

Michael J Contos

IN 1970, FIRST LIEUTENANT MICHAEL J. CONTOS GLANCES ACROSS THE FIELD WHERE HE WOULD BE LEADING HIS FIRST PLATOON OF CHARLIE COMPANY OF THE FIRST BRIGADE AND THE 25TH DIVISION NEAR THE CITY FORMERLY KNOWN AS SAIGON.

14 Comments on "Vietnam War Book Review a 4-Stars Rate!"

LaDonna Remy says:
Congratulations Michael.
Michael J. Contos, signing in as Contoveros, says the following:
Thank you. And thanks for your help to all of us who have to deal with the trauma in our lives.
LaDonna Remy says:
Thank you, Michael, that is a truly lovely compliment. ♥♥

Contoveros says:
The following are comments shared on Facebook about the review published above:
Andrea Hornett:
C O N G R A T U L A T I O N S!!
Michael J. Contos:
Thanks. It looks good in print!
So do you, come to think about…

Janet Mather:
I wish I had been so articulate! Wonderful review!
Michael J. Contos
You are perfect just the way you are!
Thanks ...

Elena Jarosz:
Applause (Hands clapping!)
Michael J. Contos
thanks for the hands clapping!

Martha Bush:
THUMBS UP
Michael J. Contos:
Best thumbs up I've seen this week!

Cliff Cutler:
Terrific Michael. Finished your book last week. Being of the same generation was very helpful.
Michael J. Contos
I'm glad you could appreciate it and share your thoughts!

Patty Kline Capaldo:
Wonderful review!
Congratulations
Michael J. Contos:

Yeah, I got a lot of encouragement from you guys to hang in there with our writing. Feels good to get positive feedback.
Patty Kline Capaldo:
can we throw a book signing party for you?
Michael J. Contos:
Yeah, why not?
I have no idea what that would be like, but what the hell. Let's go for it!
Patty Kline Capaldo:
Cool! I'll email you and we can work out the details.
Michael J. Contos:
Please do. Thanks!

Rose DeLone:
Nice!
Michael J. Contos:
Thanks. We're still waiting on your memoirs.

Regina Precise:
I'm happy for your congratulations, you know your book would make a good Christmas present
Michael J. Contos:
You got it. I'll pass one into Nick in a few weeks!

Terri Kiral:
Michael, this is so wonderful. Well-deserved. I am crying happy tears for you.
Michael J. Contos:
Terri Kiral

I feel your warmth and your joy. Writing has made me so happy to have friends like you who appreciate our efforts!

Calliope Joy:
You always are a STAR… and I believe you are the only Contoveros who went into the service unless your brothers did…
Michael J. Contos:
My brother George signed up for the army and spent 22 years as an enlisted man.
I learned only recently that he had died of Agent Orange which he received while serving in Vietnam as a combat engineer.
Calliope Joy:
WOW, a career man. How old was George when he passed?
Michael J. Contos:
George was only 55 years old. Way too young.
My mom and dad both lived until age 78, some 20 years apart.
Calliope Joy:
yes too, too young. How much older was your father from your mother?
Michael J. Contos:
Twenty years older.
They met at the New York World's Fair while he was working as a chef in the British Pavilion.
Calliope Joy:
Wow, same as my father was 20 years older than my mother. Father died at 82 in 1998, mother died at 78 in 2010
Michael J. Contos:
You got good genes!
Calliope Joy:
As do you!

Amy Nora Doyle MacLeod:
Congrats on this fabulous review. Of course, your book will be well received – a heart willing to share an intimate truth-telling of the horrors too many experienced and written with professional skills.
Thank you for all you gave and endured – including coming back home to all of us who had/have no clue!
Michael J. Contos:
Most veterans I know who faced combat don't glorify war and we hope no one would ever have to go into battle anymore....

Dolores Lukomski:
Likes you, respects you and appreciates your service and sacrifice to keep people like me safe at home.
Michael J. Contos:
Glad to have served and glad that it's over!

Frances Eberwine Holod:
THANKS FOR YOUR SERVICE. WE WERE JUST DOWN IN VIRGINIA FOR THE TOMB OF THE UNKNOWN SOLDIER AND BROTHER JIM PLACED A WREATH ON IT FOR A VIETNAM VET. IT WAS WONDERFUL TO BE THERE AND WATCH SOME FRIENDS LAYING THE WREATH AND RAISING MONEY FOR THE MEMORIAL FOR THIS SOLDIER IN ATLANTIC CITY. I WILL SEND THE LINK TO YOU IF YOU WOULD LIKE TO SEE SOME OF THE PICTURES.
Michael J. Contos:
Our generation will never forget our fallen soldiers. Even those we may not yet know of their identity. I lost my dog tags in the war zone and I don't know how they could have identified my remains with no dental work done in the army.

Let me know more about the link you mentioned.
Thanks!
Michael J. Contos:
Thanks again!
Frances Eberwine Holod:
ON MONDAY THE 25TH JIM AND CHERIE HAVE BY INVITATION GONE TO THE SHIP THAT BROUGHT HOME THE UNKNOWN SOLDIER IN PHILADELPHIA
Michael J. Contos:
I salute all of them!
Thank you.

Frank Warner:
Mike, you deserve a 21-gun salute for the book, like the salute you got from your men. You did your duty and did it well.
I was struck by your description, on that 'worst day,' of the wounded soldier screaming until you looked at him and then screaming again when you looked away. It shows the faith these guys put in their lieutenants, and yes, reflects the faith that children place in their parents.
I remember you saying, years ago, how the Animals' "We Gotta Get Out of This Place!" Was such a popular song in Vietnam. Now I understand that better.
By the way, your book mentions the movie "Captain Newman M.D." with Gregory Peck starring as an army psychiatrist. I was a 10-year-old living there in Fort Huachuca when they filmed the movie. I didn't see Gregory Peck, but I did see a crew filming part of the Eddie Albert suicide scene at the water tower. Albert wasn't there at the time; the crew threw a dummy off the tower to get the crowd reaction below.
Great book, Mike. You put your heart and soul into it. May you never have to drink an air-dropped Fanta soda!
Michael J. Contos:
Fanta soda sucked then - and it still sucks today.

Yeah, when that young soldier, who incidentally had only joined our platoon that day, stopped crying when I spoke to him as his commanding officer, I felt a connection to ease the pain long enough for him to hear me and take in the fact that help was in its way to medivac him out of there.

You don't have to have faced a battle to show what horrors stay with some people who saw combat. The movie "Captain Newman M.D." captured it. I had forgotten the part played by Eddie Albert and am concerned for the vets from our latest wars who are dealing with the trauma.

Thanks for the salute, you old Nader's Raider good buddy.

Ron Landsel:
Thanks Michael.
Michael J. Contos:
"I ain't gonna study war no more" was the refrain I seem to recall a bunch of veterans sang at a meditation retreat.
Sound familiar?
It should be a guiding principle for all veterans of all wars!

Carmen Suarez says:
What a GREAT review! Fantastic. I'm also so happy for you. Becoming a published author is no small thing, but putting your story out there is incredible. And what an amazing story it is.
Contoveros says:
Yes, being published is a rare treat that few people will actually pursue in their lifetimes, Thank you for your encouraging words!

Mike Sangiacomo says:

Nice work Mike. You never talked about those days when we were at the newspaper, we didn't push. Look forward to reading it. Mike

<u>Contoveros</u> says:
Yeah, I never brought the war up except with some veterans who I covered for The Mercury newspaper.
I remember a few old-timers from Pottstown. They were members of what was called the "Last Man's Club." It was a small group of World War I veterans who had purchased a very expensive bottle of wine. The man who lived the longest got to drink the bottle in memory of his comrades.
Never did a follow-up to the late 1970s story but always wondered who was the winner …

<u>Grandfathersky</u> says:
Michael – congratulations are in order for publishing, for sharing these years of your life with us. Telling the story is vital to the healing, something I know you worked long and hard to find (and I am sure continues to this day) … Peter

<u>Contoveros</u> says:
Yes, writing is therapeutic and there is a healing process that takes place as you well know.
It only took me 50 years to get it out of my system and into a book form. It feels good to have finally completed the mission.

<u>Grandfathersky</u> says:
Michael – So many thoughts reading this, but one just came up I should share – page 113 – between those "butter bars" were the blank lines of the pages yet to be written in your life. We can never know the meaning until the ink fills our pages …

<u>Contoveros</u> says:
Who knows what – – – – lurks in the hearts of man?
Yes, there could be something more to write about. As one of my mother's favorite crooners – Al Jolson – once said: "You ain't seen nothin' yet."

<u>Grandfathersky</u> says:

Keep going! Your writing style reflects your time in journalism, and putting yourself "out there" I'm sure has created a mirror for you to reflect on. I know I've used the term Bodhisattva before. After reading this, it appears you gave up much to protect the souls in your charge then, and still. I think your platoon putting on their own salute shows their understanding of this … You've given much, and deserve much!

<u>Contoveros</u> says:

I am honored and humbled by your kind words.

You try to do your best and hope for guidance along the path and sometimes it comes in the form of a fellow blogger like yourself.

Thanks, my good friend!

www.ingramcontent.com/pod-product-compliance
Lightning Source LLC
Chambersburg PA
CBHW071140090426
42736CB00012B/2176